Letters to Australia

Julius Stone at the ABC microphone.

Letters to Australia

The Radio Broadcasts (1942–72)

Essays from 1956–1972, Volume 6

Julius Stone

Edited by Jonathan Stone, Eleanor (Stone) Sebel, and Michael E Stone

SYDNEY UNIVERSITY PRESS

First published in 2019 by Sydney University Press

© Jonathan Stone, Eleanor (Stone) Sebel and Michael E Stone 2019
© Sydney University Press 2019

Fisher Library F03
University of Sydney NSW 2006
AUSTRALIA
Email: sup.info@sydney.edu.au
sydneyuniversitypress.com.au

A catalogue record for this book is available from the National Library of Australia.

ISBN 9781743326114 paperback
ISBN 9781743326572 epub
ISBN 9781743326589 mobi

Cover image by Ulf Kaiser, pen and ink on cardboard. This sketch was created in 1992, when it appeared in the *Australian*, with a review by Gordon Hawkins of a biography of Julius Stone by Leonie Star. The editors are grateful to the artist for his permission to reproduce the sketch here.

Cover design by Miguel Yamin

The last time our forebears took too big a bite at knowledge, they were expelled from the Garden of Eden. Adam was told he would henceforth eat only by the sweat of his brow, and Eve that she would in sorrow bring forth children.

This century of humankind has, for the first time, the chance to overcome this divine punishment by using knowledge of earthly tasks, like feeding the hungry, healing the sick and taking the sweat and agony out of human labour. We are in a position to transform the earth into which our ancestors were banished into a warm and gracious home for all their children.

From 'Space Programs of the Great Powers'

Questions are now being raised about Australia's attitude in case political and military collapses in South Vietnam produce a flood of refugees seeking to escape from political reprisals by a victorious north. These are ... questions of plain humanity towards persons faced with death or degradation unless they are given a new home. Australia should join vigorously with other humane communities in relieving its share of this tragedy.

From 'Calwell and Chipp Clash Over Multiculturalism; The Politics of Immigration'

Contents

Contents

Editors' Preface

This is the preface to four volumes (3–6) of *Letters to Australia*. Their appearance completes the publication of the radio broadcasts of our father Julius Stone, which went to air between 1942 and 1972. As we noted in Volumes 1 and 2, the manuscripts of the talks lay in the National Library and National Archives of Australia for 20 years after his death in 1985, until we 'discovered' them there (we all have memories of hearing them as children), sensed their quality and contemporary relevance, and determined to make them available using today's media; in short to publish them.

The period of the talks spanned their author's time at the University of Sydney, where he held the Challis Chair of International Law and Jurisprudence. He published extensively in those fields of learning, gaining wide international repute. But even as he wrote the profound and contemplative analyses of law that gained him that reputation, he also extended his mind to contemporary events in the immediate world – the aftermath of World War II, the emergence of the Cold War, the conflicts in Korea and Indochina and the Middle East, and the establishment and significance of multi-lateral bodies, particularly the UN, by which the postwar generations sought to limit war; and much more.

He found outlet for these analyses in commentary programs of the Australian Broadcasting Commission, five to 15 minute slots called *News Commentary, News Review, World Affairs* and *Notes on the News*. Today he would have been a blogger; then his pleasure was real when some stranger recognised his rich and distinctive voice or corresponded with him, and he knew that, however alone he was in the broadcast studio, people heard and listened.

Did he have a program in these talks? An aim to be achieved? Each reader can judge that; to his editors and children, he wrote them in the belief that only the human intellect – armed with knowledge of the vast history of human endeavour, success and failure – could forge a world freer of the conflict that had made the first half of the 20th century so terrible. Comprehensive understanding of human history and rigorous analysis of the human present – these he sought to contribute to the postwar world. No less, nor more.

So these essays were a contemporary complement to the more timeless analyses of human law encompassed in his disciplines of jurisprudence and international law. The present four volumes add just over 400 essays to the 185 published in 2014.

Though the immediate events that stimulated these talks are past, the dominant themes of the talks – the balancing of international power, relaxing the fears of nations while being hard-headed about how nations behave, basing judgement of issues on both learning and compassion for the human state, great power interactions and the management of extremism – are all still relevant. The more so in a time when the claims of nations are so often based on self-serving interpretations of the present and the past, bolstered by misuse of agreed international law. So we committed ourselves to their transcription from decades-old typescript, and to the detailed editing required, a task that we began in 2006.

These four volumes are dedicated, as were Volumes 1 and 2, to Zena Sachs LLB who, as our father's colleague of 40 years, typed most of the original talks and, after his death, ensured the safe storage of the great majority in his papers in the National Library of Australia. A minor part of the opus was placed in Australia's National Archives, presumably by the Australian Broadcasting Commission.

Readers of Volumes 1 and 2 will note one difference in the layout of these four volumes. We have not attempted the thematic organisation used in the earlier volumes; in these last four volumes, the talks are presented in chronological order. A thematic layout was not possible because, particularly in the longer (15 minute) talks, he began to deal with more than one topic. As previously, our editing has been minimal, excluding only a few talks for which part of the typescript was lost and, in the remainder, only a very occasional intervention for the sake of clarity and for consistency in abbreviations and titles.

Finally, a note concerning Julius Stone's voice, part of any broadcaster's persona. We have located several high quality recordings of him speaking on the ABC, in the National Archives of Australia. None were of the broadcasts in the *Letters to Australia* sequence. One is a reflective comment, recorded in the 1980s, about the first of the broadcasts, the wartime broadcasts presented in Volume 1; the others are also from the early 1980s, comments on contemporary legal issues. We hope to make them available to the public in the future.

We are indebted to Sydney University Press for its long commitment to this project. The University of Sydney was his professional home for the major part of his career (he had trained at Oxford and Harvard Universities and was Dean of Law at Auckland before coming to Sydney in late 1941); it is fitting that their publication comes from SUP. We are also indebted to Ms Charean Adams, who saw the task of transcription through from beginning to end, to the Director of the Julius Stone Institute, Dr Kevin Walton, for his continuing support, and to Sydney University Press, for their skilled assistance in publication.

Jonathan Stone
Eleanor (Stone) Sebel
Michael Stone
Sydney, 2017

US Senate Challenges President on Aid; H-tests and Peaceful Uses of Atomic Energy

Monday 9 January 1956, 1.15pm 2BL

The challenge thrown out to President Eisenhower by the Democrat leader of the Senate, and Chairman of the Foreign Relations Committee, Senator George, this weekend, is of epochal importance. Its outcome may determine the whole future of Western relations with Asia, and indeed with all underdeveloped areas of the world.

The President, in last week's State of the Union message to Congress appealed for special authority for programs of economic aid to the free world for a number of years, and he is due shortly to elaborate his proposals on this to Congress.

Senator George's challenge goes to two points. First, he opposes any further extension of economic as distinct from merely military aid. Second, he opposes the authorisation of aid for any period longer than a year; for he thinks that Congress should be able to review the aid program every year.

On both points, it seems to me, Senator George is placing the Democratic Party across the path of real American leadership in the present phase of the East-West struggle for influence in the yet uncommitted areas of the world.

Mr Eisenhower's present proposal is itself a courageous reversal of what many thinkers, including myself, regarded as a great error of the mid-century year. About 1949, the policy of economic aid was largely replaced in American planning by the policy of mutual aid. Instead of aid to re-establish and raise collapsed living standards, Congress decided that aid should rather go to peoples willing to use it for building military strength for resistance to communist aggression.

Since 1949 there has been a radical shift in the ratios of American economic and military aid to the rest of the world. According to the Randall Commission on Foreign Economic Policy, out of total aid of $41.7 billion from 1949 to 1953, $33 billion were for economic aid, and only $8.7 billion for military aid – that is, only about 20 percent was for military aid. But in 1954, $53 out of $73 billion – or 73 percent – was for military aid. This change of emphasis, to military aid, has been a double handicap to Western policy. Many Asian countries for example, which felt the need for peaceable economic aid in quantities not available through such modest schemes such as the Colombo Plan and the Point Four Program, have become sitting birds for communist economic influence.

In the middle of last year, Peking announced a program of economic aid to small Asian states, and both Peking and Moscow made grants to Vietnam, and this trickle has spread into a Soviet propaganda flood, which now covers India, Indonesia, Burma, the Middle East, and now, according to the weekend cables, even the remote African Republic of Liberia.

Moreover, this American switch to military aid gave great plausibility to the Soviet propaganda claim that America and the West were using Asian countries as cat's-paws in imperialistic and militaristic plans to suppress Asian nationalist movements; that aid from the West had military strings attached, and was not worth having.

While communist grants in aid are still insignificant compared with the magnificent proportions of American Marshall Aid, Moscow has made them with such a flourish of disinterested generosity, that they are already winning the propaganda initiative on this economic front.

Undoubtedly, these plain facts have something to do with the President's present determination to shift the balance of aid to Asia back to economic and away from military aid – back to the Marshall Aid of the days before Mutual Aid.

Why the Democrats should be so sternly opposed to this is by no means obvious in terms of foreign policy. Marshall Aid was a Democratic notion after all, and we have been accustomed to think of the Republicans rather than the Democrats as the short-sighted illiberals of foreign policy. I suspect that Senator George in his stand will not have the overall support of other Democratic leaders like Adlai Stevenson. If I prove wrong on this, it will be because Senator George's stand is a mere manoeuvre in domestic party politics in a presidential election year – an attempt to win the support of corporations for a policy of lower taxation.

And of course, Senator George's further point – that economic aid should be authorised only from year to year, thus forbidding any long foreign policy planning, – aggravates the ill impact of his stand on American world leadership.

For I would like to add that President Eisenhower's new proposal has more potential significance than as a mere revival of the Marshall Aid. For that plan was after all a grand and generous but temporary measure of emergency relief for postwar economic distress.

This postwar distress has now happily disappeared in most countries. A great program of economic aid at this stage would go far, along with lesser ventures such as Colombo Plan aid, to establish the principle of international collective economic responsibility for the welfare of the less privileged peoples of the world. Compared with the potentialities of this principle, the Marshall and Colombo Plans may someday look rather like the soup kitchens of 1929 in relation to state welfare.

It is some comfort that news of the two projected American hydrogen bomb explosions in the Pacific is accompanied by important steps in the peaceful use of atomic energy. The first American atomic power plant on a commercial basis seems to have passed its initial tests; France's commercial reactor is well advanced; and America has announced that it has selected Manila in the Philippines as the site for its nuclear reactor training centre under the Colombo Plan. The selection will no doubt cause some heartburn in centres like Ceylon, which had hoped to provide the site; but it is quite understandable, even if it is not the best public relations, for Washington to prefer a site that is protected by some of its strongest military disposition in the Far East.

Apart from the usual tragicomical boasting about how big a bang they are going to make, the two H-bombs now to be exploded are notable since they are to be carried by aircraft. The H-bombs hitherto exploded at Eniwetok have been too heavy to be carried by air; so I should guess was the bomb recently exploded by the Soviet Union. If the new experiments succeed therefore, they will mark an important stage in the emergence of the H-bomb as a practical weapon and, unless the two sides keep their heads steady, in the human descent into an overwhelming bonfire.

SEATO and Australian Foreign Policy

Sunday 22 January 1956, Australia and the World, 2FC

Reports say that the SEATO conference of military advisers in Melbourne finally dropped into low gear on a number of military problems because of conflict between the British 'speak softly' policy and the American 'stand up and be counted' policy in Southeast Asia, and that the unsettled questions will be sent forward to the SEATO foreign ministers in Karachi next March.

The British, it is said, continue to urge SEATO members to avoid sabre-rattling or any action that might offend or incite communists to new aggression or destroy the chance of Peking developing an independent foreign policy; while the Americans favour a campaign to show that the Manila Pact members are ready to fight aggression and to induce other Asian states to join SEATO.

No member is more deeply concerned than Australia in the outcome of these debates, for – in theory at any rate – the Southeast Asia Collective Defence Organisation (SEATO's full name) should be the central pillar of Australia's security.

The Commonwealth government, as Mr Menzies pointed out last year, while it supports the United Nations, has no illusions on this point. It was, he said, on SEATO that Australia was primarily relying, for the UN Charter is no substitute for power.

SEATO itself is based on the Manila Treaty of 1954. In original conception it was to have had a broad foundation of Asian members; but in the final result the only Asian participants are the Philippines, Pakistan and Thailand, though the treaty may, in certain circumstance, be extended to cover Laos, Vietnam and Cambodia.

Obviously, in these circumstances, the brunt of any military preparations or activity that may become involved must fall on the Western states participating, notably the United States, the United Kingdom, France, Australia and New Zealand. And this represents a double weakness from the Western standpoint. Not only are the resources of the strongest Asian powers, such as India, not available; but in addition, the dominant military role of the Western powers makes SEATO a plausible target for communist allegations that SEATO is a mere instrument of Western military policy.

It is not surprising, therefore, that, from its birth, some of the basic aspects of SEATO have been controversial, even between SEATO members. First, there has been disagreement as to whether SEATO was directed against any aggression in the area, or only against communist aggression. While the treaty is drawn in general terms, the United States attached to its signature a reservation limiting its own participation to resistance to communist aggression. This could obviously become a vital matter for Australia, since we cannot easily forget that Japan in the last war came very near to invading our shores, and no realist could honestly exclude the possibility that such an adventure might sometime be repeated.

If it were repeated, Australia would not strictly be entitled to call on American military aid under the SEATO treaty. She would then have to rely on the earlier ANZUS Treaty, that is, the mutual security treaty between the United States, Australia and New Zealand, under which an attack on any of the parties from any source in the Pacific would activate the obligations of mutual defence. This, indeed, would seem to be the only respect in which the ANZUS Treaty still remains of strictly military importance to Australia; for all other practical military purposes SEATO has replaced it.

Of course, the ANZUS Treaty still maintains substantial political importance, since the regular meetings of the ANZUS Council provide us with a forum in which Australian leaders can make their voice heard by Washington on Pacific planning and strategy, in which they can keep Australian interests before Washington, and have access to the thinking and planning of the American administration.

A second major focus of controversy in the history of SEATO has been as to whether it should be modelled on NATO, or remain a much looser organisation. Is it, in other words, to be built into a collective military machine, with its own staff organisation, forces and equipment, poised for collective defence? Or is it to be merely a consultative piece of machinery, which will only develop into a mature military machine after an armed attack has occurred.

On this matter it is still by no means clear that SEATO has made up its mind. At its first council meeting at Bangkok, it established a secretariat, along with standing council representatives at Bangkok, as well as a Military Liaison Group, with various committees located elsewhere.

On the question, however, of military headquarters, Britain appears to have pressed the claims of Singapore, the United States wants Manila, resulting in a stalemate, which has thus far prevented any final decision. Mr Dulles softened America's refusal to station forces in Southeast Asia by pointing out that American forces in the Far East already embraced nearly a million men, 400 warships, and 30 air squadrons.

In a sense, therefore, SEATO has been left in a situation, which has the worst of both worlds. There is some uncertainty as to how far and how quickly the United States would actively participate in a military resistance to any merely local aggression; yet, by its military overtones, SEATO's hopes of broadening into a kind of eastern Locarno have been rather blighted. The possibility, for example, of Indian participation is no longer even discussed.

Nevertheless, of course, considerable importance attaches to the advance planning which goes on in the council, the Military Liaison Group, and the committees of SEATO, to deal with both military and political threats in the area. And the regular meetings of well-briefed representatives of the eight governments establish a foundation on which a united command and an integrated strategy might quickly arise in case of emergency. This may not be wholly satisfying from the Australian standpoint; but Australia is, in any case, in a position very different from that of Washington or London. Washington tends to view Southeast Asia as part of its oceanic line of defence of the western United States, of which the westerly pivot is Manila in the Philippines. Southeast Asia, in other words, is, apart from the ANZUS Treaty, on the boundaries of American strategic interests. For London, on the other hand, strategic anxiety looks eastward across Africa, the Persian Gulf and the Indian Ocean, with an easterly pivot on Singapore and Malaya.

For Australia, however, Southeast Asia is not on the boundary, as it were, of her strategic interests and anxieties, but at the very heart of them. The nearness to Southeast Asia of her colonial trustee and metropolitan territories, and her gross inferiority in manpower thus spell her life and death dependence on both American and British lines of communication and power. Australia is scarcely in a position to choose between Singapore and Manila.

Again, Australia also finds it impossible to choose between the London emphasis on building political bridges with Asia regardless of ideology, and the Washington emphasis on building military ramparts against communist aggression. Our geographical position presses us towards London's desire to build comradeship with Asian peoples; but it also leads us to value almost as strongly as Washington, the strength of military ramparts in case the comradeship should fail to eventuate.

In this position, our policy-makers have tended, wherever possible, to avoid taking sides on the points of policy in debate between London and Washington, and our military assistance in Malaya has had to be channelled other than through SEATO. There is little doubt, however, that much heart-searching must lie ahead for Canberra on many of these questions, not the least of which may involve a thorough reappraisal of the military and non-military components in our strategic security.

SEATO Debates; Eisenhower Defends His Secretary of State; Australia and GATT

Monday 23 January 1956, Notes on the News, 1.15pm 2BL

It is related that the great Einstein was asked one day why man, with a brain marvellous enough to solve the deepest problems of the physical universe, was unable to rid himself of the fear and danger of war. The answer is clear, said Einstein, in his direct and simple way – 'physics is easier than politics.'

And when you come down to analyse why political problems are so hard, the most important reason is that no one can ever know with certainty which course was the correct one to take until long after he has taken it, and that even then, he can only make an arguable guess about it, and very often not even that.

Take, for example, the conflicting views as to the attitude that the West should be adopting towards East and Southeast Asia, which are reported to have put into low gear last week's SEATO conference in Melbourne. The communiqué after the conference seems to be more eloquent in what it omits than in what it includes. According to unofficial reports, the American delegation thought that the best course at this juncture was to launch a political campaign around the slogan that SEATO is ready to meet all aggression, and that all Asian states which do not want to be swallowed up by aggressors should join SEATO.

The British delegation, however, appeared to think that rather than the best, this might be the worst possible course. For it might simply give plausibility to the Moscow and Peking propaganda line that SEATO is merely the instrument of a new form of Western imperialism. For it would mean that the West would seem to be trying to force military commitments on the uncommitted Asian states, while Moscow and Peking preached peace and made no military demands.

British counsel at Melbourne, therefore, was that SEATO should speak softly to Asia, avoiding any open advocacy of warlike solutions in advance of the actual crises of aggression.

To me personally, the British standpoint appears obviously more realistic. Yet I find it quite impossible to think of any arguments by which I could demonstrate this beyond doubt to anyone convinced of the American view. No one could do more in advance than make a guess. Even, indeed, if we waited ten years after adopting the British view, and if there had been no further aggression in Asia in the meanwhile, that would not prove that the American standpoint was wrong, or that it would not have been equally effective in preventing aggression.

In actuality, of course, since neither country will wholly abandon its viewpoint, each of them has a complete explanation, in case aggression does recur in Asia, as to why its policy did not prevent it.

In the President's first press conference since the crisis in his health he took a balanced view of the international position. He also defended Mr Dulles against recent press attacks on his 'brink of war' propositions in *Life* magazine. He said that Mr Dulles was the best Secretary of State he had known, but the President was also careful to sit on the fence about the *Life* article, claiming that he had not read it.

He did, however, make one point, which may go to the very heart of the 'brink of war' controversy. What has been mainly criticised in the *Life* article is that it was open to the interpretation that it was on deliberate American planning that the world had come to the brink of war in recent times, and Mr Dulles was proud of this as a sample of supreme 'diplomatic art'. The criticism is not only that this is melodramatic egoism on the part of Mr Dulles, but also that it is very bad public relations for Washington vis-à-vis her allies and the neutralist peoples of Asia.

The President pointed out that if a country stood firm on any policy, that always brought it to the 'brink of something', because you could not control the reaction of the opponent.

In that sense, a foreign policy can lead to the brink of war and yet remain justifiable in terms of the policy on which you are standing firm, and the balancing of the chances of compromise and success or war and failure.

Obviously, then, to go to the brink and yet not over it, is not just a matter of anyone's courage or failure; it is above all a question of whether both sides have sufficiently good reasons for not pushing each other over the brink.

In other words, the central fact of the present world situation since 1951 has been military stalemate. Brink of war situations are merely situations in which the fists are openly brandished on both sides. The fact that war doesn't come, however, is not a result of the brandishing; it is finally a result of the military stalemate. The supreme diplomatic art in such a situation is not the fist-shaking, but the finding of compromises of concrete conflicts of interests, which will make it safer to put human hands back to more peaceful uses for longer and longer intervals.

Comparative lack of interest by Australia in the coming fourth international conference of the General Agreement on Tariffs and Trade (GATT) is a remarkable contrast to our rather intense attitude to last year's session for the review of the General Agreement.

This year the leader of the delegation, Mr HFB Heyes, has told the opening session that Australia's position as a supplier is not likely to lead to tariff adjustments; especially since in agricultural products, Australia's major export concern, tariffs were only one form, and not the most important, of protection.

Mr Heyes could have added that Australia regards herself as still engaged in absorbing concessions obtained last year at the Review Conference, when her special position as a country of high living standards, rapid industrial development, as well as dependence on exports of primary products, was recognised. The resulting 1955 concessions permitted freer use of tariff policy to encourage Australia's rapid development and freer use of import restrictions to balance payments, and gave some safeguards against the threat from mass disposal of agricultural surpluses, especially by the United States.

Western Diplomacy and the Strategy of Deterrence

Sunday 3 May 1959, Australia and the World, 12.45 pm 2BL

Western foreign ministers, including new Secretary of State Herter, after a meeting only half the expected length, declared on Thursday that they were fully agreed on a common Western front towards the meetings between them and the Soviet Foreign minister, beginning 11 May.

The central problem in these talks was created by Moscow's declared intention of transferring its power in East Berlin to the East German authorities, and thus compelling the Western powers to deal with East Germany for maintaining access to the West Berlin enclave, across the 100-mile-wide corridor of communist-dominated territory.

This, however, is but an over-simplified version of the Berlin crisis. The West German government, for example, feels that the entire questions of German reunification, German disarmament, and German alignments are involved. It squarely rejects the central Soviet plan for reunification by negotiation with East Germany, and insists on all-German free elections as the basis.

Broadly, de Gaulle shares the West German positions. From the present French standpoint, within a hoped-for European Community, France does not want Germany neutralised. This, of course, is in strong contrast with traditional French attitudes; but French Foreign Minister de Murville affirmed it again as late as last Wednesday.

The British approach has been dominated by the view that thermonuclear conflict in Europe must destroy Britain, and in very quick time. A cynic might say that Mr Macmillan is only optimistic about negotiating with Russia because he is so pessimistic about the consequences for Britain of refusal to negotiate each East-West issue as it become critical.

The Prime Minister's view is that the West will have cards to play at the coming conferences, if it is prepared and able to broaden the issues to include a phased program of disengagement of Western and Soviet forces in Central Europe, following on German reunification by graduated stages, including free elections. There have also been British suggestions that a renewed Western acceptance of entrenched Soviet influence throughout its satellite world is a card worth playing.

The American position is reputed to waver between those of its allies. The less charitable have pointed out that there is no clear cut American position, beyond the President's warning that the use of thermo-atomic weapons could not be ruled out if the West Berlin situation degenerated into hostilities. But it is, of course, only fair to add that the period of this Berlin crisis largely coincides with the uncertainly arising from the recurrence of Mr Dulles' grave illness, only recently ended by Mr Herter's appointment as Secretary of State.

Within these general contrasts of position lie narrower, and often bitter, issues, such as an alleged smouldering personal resentment of Chancellor Adenauer towards Britain, dating from occupation days of old, and the West German allegation that the British idea of disengagement in Central Europe would violate undertakings given to West Germany, and would undermine West Germany's whole diplomatic position.

Can we assume from Thursday's declaration that full agreement has now been reached that all of these grave differences have disappeared? I doubt this. But I also think that the deeper crisis of Western foreign policy which is symbolised in these differences is now coming to be clearly seen for the first time.

Let us try to see this deeper crisis in perspective. Broadly speaking, until the Soviet Union acquired thermonuclear weapons, the West would in theory have enforced its will on the Soviet Union. That course, however, would have involved a cold-blooded decision to destroy masses of human beings, an impossible decision for a civilised Western country to take. The Soviet offensive postures of this time might have been in part a cover for real fear of preventive war, but she was, at any rate, able to pursue her probing policies with impunity, right into the present phase of equal weaponry.

Since 1950, both sides have moved into the exposed position of two scorpions in a bottle, each capable of mortally striking the other, but only at a suicidal price. In this later period, all specific East-West conflicts have tended to merge into an overall matrix of conflicting Soviet-Western systems and ideologies.

Particularly in the West, we have tended to translate each political (and even economic) conflict into military terms. And foreign policy has increasingly taken the form of warning the adversary that massive retaliation would be our answer to specified aggressive acts, of the so-called strategy of 'the great deterrent'. Old-fashioned statecraft has been increasingly replaced by the making of military threats, and by efforts (to use the technical jargon) to make the threats 'credible' to the enemy.

But it is now tolerably clear that neither side can expect, or even hope, to achieve more than a precarious security by this strategy of deterrence. Even if tomorrow the United States found itself capable of destroying at a single surprise assault all Soviet bases capable of retaliatory action, this could not give Western security unless they were willing actually to make this assault in cold blood. Short of this, Western superiority would still be precarious; its duration would still depend on day-to-day assessment of relative technological advances, and the state of military intelligence, on the two sides.

In short, the translation of political problems which formerly were dealt with by statecraft into military problems of overall deterrent power, has reached an impasse. This, I believe, is the deeper and wider meaning of wearisome talk about summit conferences, and the stress in the foreign ministers' communiqué on Tuesday on Western will to negotiate.

Can we (and here I mean to include both sides) can we now re-translate into political terms the problems hitherto thrust into the military arena of global deterrence? Can humanity re-discover and recapture, from within the military matrix of global struggle, those skills of statecraft necessary to its survival? These are the questions for which the Geneva negotiations will be an attempt, and I pray not the last attempt, to find a favourable answer.

Menzies on the Iron Curtain; Death of Dulles; Monkeys in Space

Friday 29 May 1959, Notes on the News, 1.15pm 2BL

No one, and certainly no Australian, should underrate the significance of the speech made by Prime Minister Menzies at the luncheon just tendered him in New York by the National Press Club. The main tenor of Mr Menzies' remarks is still in the news, due both to continued press discussion, and to the fact that it is thought also to have figured in Mr Menzies' talks with Secretary of State Herter and with President Eisenhower yesterday.

The main propositions, which Mr Menzies put to the press, were unambiguous enough. First, he said, we 'can't have a permanent Iron Curtain' because in the face of modern weapons we must not breed fear, hatred and distrust into generations of men. It followed, second, that he was 'all for conferences'. He added that he ventured to say this even if it was an 'impertinent' observation for a 'travelling outsider'.

Third, he expressly rejected the view, which has been perhaps the dominant view in Washington, and especially in the vicinity of the White House, that summit meetings were dangerous for the West, since failure would do positive harm. On the contrary, he urged, a frank Western approach to summit meetings might bring real gains and need not involve any loss, even if it failed. Only the communists, he thought, could lose if, in face of a sincere Western attempt to come to terms, failure resulted from Soviet discourtesy, threats or refusal to show their real hand.

Finally, and perhaps most important of all, Mr Menzies said that 'the more I think about these matters the less I fear the physical success of the communist world and the more I fear its mental and moral success'.

In the context of the debate concerning the possibilities of a summit conference, these Australian opinions may well be deemed 'impertinent' by some Washington quarters. For after the expected Soviet rejection of the Western 'package' terms, the British policy of flexible negotiation with Moscow still stands in conflict with the French and West German policies. And, on one point at least, Washington has gone steadily with the Franco-German view, namely that the Foreign Ministers' Conference must attain some real results before a summit conference is warranted.

Mr Menzies is thus ranging himself on this matter with London rather than Washington. At least since the lamented John Foster Dulles visited Australia to persuade Canberra to make peace with Japan, I know of no major issue in which we have publicly sided with London in a controversy with Washington. And whatever the merits of the particular issue, most of us will (I think) welcome this as a sign that we might still come to have a mind of our own.

In the context of Western-Soviet competition for the approval of the so-called uncommitted nations, especially of Asia, Mr Menzies' standpoint must inevitably put Washington on notice that, however persuasively President Eisenhower might explain to Americans the reasons against a summit meeting, the reasons are likely to be ill-received elsewhere. And this, in turn, would be a reminder that military stalemate may still be accompanied by grave political losses; that – as Mr Menzies put it – we ought to fear Soviet mental and moral success even more than their physical success.

Certainly, the President is entitled to resent Soviet attempts to force him to the summit by threats of producing a fait accompli in Berlin. But neither would it be reasonable, on the other hand, to expect Moscow, in advance of the summit conference, to accept the Western plan. What would be reasonable is a moratorium on all Berlin developments pending an early conference.

Yesterday incidentally, was 27 May, and this you may recall was the first date projected by Mr Khrushchev for his Berlin showdown; he later modified it in comedian-like style to the 27 August or the 27th of some other month. And the comedy has its tragic ironies when we recall that by a decree which neither Washington nor Moscow could control, 27 May turned out to be quite a different kind of showdown – the funeral of John Foster Dulles, attended by all the foreign ministers, including Mr Gromyko. When Deputy Premier Mikoyan declared in Moscow that Mr Dulles was 'a great statesman', whose strong partisanship the Soviet preferred to 'the smooth and unintelligent', this was a tribute to the Great Leveller whose faits accomplis surpass even those of Stalin and Khrushchev.

It is not clear as yet what significance is to be attached to the informal conference of the Big Four Foreign Ministers with President Eisenhower at the White House. This may have been a merely casual initiative of the President, taking advantage of their presence for Mr Dulles' funeral. Or it may represent the kind of dramatic reappraisal, which is manifested in the diplomatic level by the recall of ambassadors for consultations with their home governments. We will probably not know till well after the foreign ministers resume their talks in Geneva, this time happily (we hope) really in private.

Meanwhile, two female monkeys, Abel and Baker, propelled 300 miles upwards towards space in the nose of Cape Canaveral's latest 52-ton 10,000 miles an hour Jupiter inter-continental rocket, are making history, with as much or as little sophistication as most of their reputed descendants. The recovery of the nose cone by craft waiting within ten miles of the end of its 1500-mile flight is a great American achievement. It marks an important stage in discovering (in official terms) whether men can act normally in space.

As you know, German scientists had much to do with the launchings both of the Soviet Sputnik and the American Explorer 1. And it is related that when in their vast orbits in space, Sputnik and Explorer finally approached each other, Sputnik leaned over confidentially towards Explorer's ear, and whispered: 'Now that we're alone, let's talk German.'

I like to think that when these two monkeys got a little away from our atmosphere, Abel too leaned over to Baker, and said confidentially, 'Now that we're alone, let's talk Monkey-Sense'.

Adenauer, the Presidency of West Germany, and the Status of East Germany

Wednesday 10 June 1959, Notes on the News, 1.15pm 2BL

Dr Erhard, Chancellor Adenauer's Minister for Economics, is hurriedly flying back to Germany from Washington because of the threatening crisis with regard to the West German presidency.

In April it was headline news that Chancellor Adenauer, after a hectic series of conferences, had decided himself to run in the presidential election in July. This was sensational because, while the Chancellorship is the highest political office, corresponding to Prime Minister, the presidency had up till then been regarded as honorific and ceremonial, and not policy making. The dignified President Heuss, who has now served for the maximum ten-year period permitted by the Constitution, had certainly acted on this assumption.

Prior to April, Chancellor Adenauer had seemed to be grooming Dr Erhard as the prospective Christian Democrat candidate in the race for President. And the result of the race was by no means sure as against the popular Social Democrat candidate, Professor Carlo Schmid.

The exact reasons for Adenauer's switch in April to be the candidate himself are still a matter of speculation. Certainly, Adenauer was the only candidate likely to defeat Social Democrat Schmid; yet he is 83 years old, which entitles him to a rest. But not the least startling part of his declaration of candidacy in April was his assertion of the view that the presidential office had more political importance than was supposed. He implied that as President he intended to continue his political activity, especially on foreign policy.

It was not unexpected, therefore, that the respected President Heuss should have taken all this as implying that he (President Heuss) had not made the most of his office; and it has been only natural therefore to find Heuss looking rather dimly on Adenauer's views, even publicly saying so.

Now, barely two months later, the Chancellor has induced his Party, with still greater difficulty than was involved in supporting him for the presidency, to reverse the April decision. He now wishes to remain Chancellor, and not to run for the presidency. The shock was sufficient, apparently, to raise reports yesterday that his own Christian Democrat Party leaders might consult with the Opposition Social Democrat leader Ollenhauer concerning the mix-up.

Presumably this switch back would mean that Dr Erhard, instead of being slated to succeed Adenauer as Chancellor, will now revert to candidacy for the presidency. For this, as I have already said, Erhard's chances are by no means certain; and in any case Erhard is rather young to be thinking of moving upstairs, out of politics. All in all, Erhard made it very clear and very public before he left the United States, that he was not at all pleased with developments.

No doubt there is a great deal of local personalities and party politics in all this; but I suspect it also has important foreign policy meaning. For instance, Dr Erhard is generally opposed to the economic integration of West Germany into Western Europe; and since he is the main architect of the German economic miracle, it might be expected that he would not, as Chancellor, be as Western-minded in this respect as Chancellor Adenauer. This is at least one point at which Opposition Social Democrat foreign policy, which favours a less committed position between Russia and the West, and more bargaining with both sides, may make contact with the Christian Democratic discontent.

The story may thus be that two months ago, when he opted for the presidency, Adenauer thought that he could build up that office sufficiently to maintain his own foreign policy line; and that his present switch back is due to the doubts later cast on this by President Heuss. He has concluded that only by remaining Chancellor can he effectively hold the reins.

All this is related, on a long-term view, to the present Four-Power negotiations concerning the future of West Germany and West Berlin. The foreign ministers' secret talks after returning from Mr Dulles' funeral have really remained secret. And consequently, speculation about the meaning of the sudden conference of the East German leaders with Mr Khrushchev in Moscow is rather at large. Reports yesterday took the line that the Russians are about to hand over communications in West Berlin to the East German regime as a fait accompli to force a summit conference, and that the West will refuse to go to the summit on this basis. This morning's cables still suggest, however, that the Moscow talks may be concerned with procuring East German agreement for some new idea to break the deadlock.

Conceivably both these lines of speculation may be correct. For instance, it may be that whilst the Russians handed over their occupation authority, the Western powers would insist on treating the East German government as merely a Soviet agent, and on continuing to hold the Soviet government responsible. And if each side then tolerated the other's position, this would be a kind of temporary de facto accommodation, with mutual face-saving, pending the projected summit conference.

In other words, even if the Four-Power communiqué contains no express agreement on the Berlin question, the foreign ministers may still have reached a measure of agreement on the broader issues behind that question.

On the Soviet side, the basic objective seems to be to get assurances that the West will cease to beam its various anti-communist activities at the Soviet buffer areas in Europe, including East Germany. On the Western side, the main objective remains, after all, to give Western Europe as a whole sufficient relief from fear of Soviet military penetration to allow them to continue building their economic strength, and to consolidate the movement for west European integration.

Agreement on this kind of level is rather too delicate a matter, especially for the West, to be baldly announced in a communiqué. And we may only be able to detect whether it has been reached by the degree of damping down of mutual recrimination over Berlin, pending the summit conference. Meanwhile, pressmen are likely to be blowing hot and cold for quite a while in order to cover any eventuality.

Two short points on weapons. One touches the lingering Geneva Conference on the possibilities of a nuclear test ban. Current reports are that the conference is just about 'on its last lap', with little chance of spectacular success. The main obstacle is, of course, the absence of any fool-proof means by which each side can detect all tests made by the other side. But it is still possible that agreement may be reached to ban only those tests which can be detected by other nations. A ban, in other words on only those tests which can't be kept secret.

And this would not be quite as silly as it sounds. For the test ban negotiations have two distinct objectives. One is disarmament – a military problem; the other is to keep radioactive fallout over the globe below danger level – a civilian public health objective. While a ban limited to tests that cannot be kept secret would not help disarmament, it might do a great deal to check radioactive fallout.

The other point is on the new US ballistic missile submarine 'George Washington', whose launching was reported in the morning cables. When completed next year, along with eight others, this submarine will be capable of cruising below surface at high speeds for indefinite times without refuelling, and of dispatching guided Polaris nuclear missiles from under water over a range of 12,000 miles.

The importance of this submarine is that for the time being it provides a mobile base for intermediate ballistic missile assault on the enemy, a base which is not vulnerable to atomic destruction by the enemy. As was brought home by the recent infra-navigation of the polar ice pack by the atomic submarine Nautilus, there is no saying where such a craft is likely to pop up next. To that extent, a Power equipped with enough of these submarines has an assurance that its whole retaliatory power cannot be wiped out by a single surprise attack by the enemy on its homeland. And since the enemy also knows this, the temptation to gamble on a surprise attack is proportionately reduced. And that has a welcome stabilising influence in a complex and ever-changing balance of atomic power.

Chinese Policy in Tibet; The Search for Co-operation in Antarctica

Monday 26 October 1959, Notes on the News, 1.15pm 2BL

On Thursday, Indian delegate Menon explained to the General Assembly why his government refused to vote for a resolution approved by 45 votes to nine, expressing grave concern at events in Tibet, and calling for respect for human rights there. Everyone knew that this was aimed at Chinese policy in Tibet, but the Indian government limited itself to hoping that changes there would take place with less cruelty, and through reconciliation.

Even as these soothing words were being reported in Peking, Chinese communist troops on India's North Kashmir border with Tibet were engaged in activity which resulted in clashes with Indian patrols, on the Indian side of the border. You may remember that it is less than two months since the near crisis caused by alleged Chinese encroachments in the same district of Ladakh, inside the Kashmir frontier, and near the India-protected states of Sikkim and Bhutan, further east on India's northern frontier with Tibet. In the present affair, 17 Indian border police were killed and several more injured or missing. While the army is now in charge at the frontier, much of the patrol work is still in the hands of the police.

In terms of loss of life, therefore, this is the most serious incident to date, and the Indian protest has indicated that she will, in due course, claim compensation for the losses involved.

The present incident is also the clearest illustration that so-called cartographical aggression is a more dangerous game than Ludo or even Monopoly. India has long resented the circulation of official Peking maps showing the Indian frontier well inside what India regards as well within her territory – to the tune, it is said, of about 32,000 square miles.

Peking claims that the place where the Indian police died was on the very border, and that it arose from an attempted incursion by a band of 70 Indian police into Chinese territory. India's protest, on the other hand, claims that the incident occurred during a search for two missing patrolmen, at a place no less than 40 miles (some reports say 80 miles) within Indian territory. Mr Nehru told parliament yesterday that while the position was a matter for great anxiety, he did not think it would lead to war; and he still calls for restraint and warns Indians against being swept by emotion.

If, as is reported, Mr Khrushchev attempted during his recent visit to persuade Chinese leaders to desist from policies which would undermine his efforts to relax international tension in preparation for a summit conference, these events do not show any encouraging response from Peking. They seem indeed, both pointless and perverse, however you look at them; no state, and no national leader, has shown a warmer sympathy with Communist China than India under Nehru and Krishna Menon. The contemptuous attitude manifest in these Chinese probings on India's northern frontiers is not only a blow at India's international prestige. It is also a serious embarrassment to Mr Nehru and Mr Menon.

As a matter of fact, the last border crisis produced an internal governmental crisis in India in which Commander-in-Chief Thimayya actually resigned due to disagreements with Foreign Minister Menon.

The 12-state Antarctic Conference, of Argentina, Australia, Belgium, Britain, Chile, France, Japan, New Zealand, Norway, South Africa, Russia and the United States ran into difficulties this weekend. It is now expected to last a month, rather than the fortnight originally planned.

The conference originated more than a year ago, during the Geophysical Year, when President Eisenhower proposed it as a means of ensuring that this vast uninhabited area be used only for peaceful purposes. Australia and other states having territorial claims there, as well as other interested states like the Soviet Union and the United States, which refuse to recognise any such claims, agreed to the conference on a basis of a very important understanding laid down by the President. This was that 'the legal status quo' in Antarctica should be frozen.

A preliminary working party of the states concerned met on and off for 15 months to prepare for the conference. They prepared a draft of 12 articles dealing with such matters as the exclusion of military activities and installations, the policing of this and of law and order generally, accessibility of the area to scientists of all nations and co-operation in scientific work, the exploitation of mineral and marine resources, including whaling, and the development of air navigation, meteorological and telecommunication services.

In a statement at the weekend, Australian Foreign Minister Casey, who is at the conference, declared that instead of building on the proposals of the Working Party, which were acceptable to Australia, the conference had begun all over again. At the end of a week, he said, it had only agreed on two articles. One provided for Antarctica to be used only for peaceful purposes, and for an observation system to police the provision. This apparently will involve stationing observers at bases of all states operating in the area. The other concerns the exchange of plans, personnel and facilities for scientific work in the Antarctic.

I said in an earlier broadcast that we might find that there had been some cross-purposes about the effect of the conference and its treaty on legal rights of the seven states who claim sovereignty in the sectors of the Antarctic. Some of these states have wishfully assumed that President Eisenhower's statement about 'freezing the legal status quo' would amount to some kind of recognition of their claims, and perhaps even bar any new claims by other states. But from the point of view of other states, like the US and Russia themselves, who dispute the validity of these claims to sovereignty, 'the legal status quo' includes the dispute, and therefore still leaves the claims in doubt.

The course taken by the conference may still bring it up against this hurdle. If this happens, we may find, even at this stage, that it is a hurdle that cannot be negotiated. This would be a disaster in many ways, since the experiment in international co-operation in peaceful activities in Antarctica could be a most important pilot operation for similar schemes of co-operation in the exploration of outer space.

Fifteen Nations Join the UN – Implications as the UN Debates Congo; Fidel and Khrushchev Visit UN in NY

Wednesday 21 September 1960, Notes on the News, 1.15pm 2BL

At the September Ordinary Session of the General Assembly, which opened a few hours ago, 15 new members are to be admitted – Cyprus and 14 newly established African states, moving into nationhood (Congo, Cameroon, Togo, Mali, Malagasay,[1] Somalia, French Congo, Dahomey, Upper Volta, Niger, Ivory Coast, Gabon, Chad and Central African Republic).

A generation ago we used to be taught about the 'scramble for Africa' by the European powers; the historians of the future will be teaching about the scramble of the European powers out of Africa. We must hope that the scramble out of Africa will have happier consequences than the scramble into Africa. But we shall need quite a lot of faith and not a little luck for the hope to be justified.

The effect of this new increase of members on the United Nations is worth a moment's thought. Of the 82 present United Nations members, 25 are African or Asian states most of them new, ten are of the Soviet bloc, and 21 are Central and South American states. For various reasons, I have not included in the Asian figure, Malaya, Turkey, the Philippines, Japan and Israel, which are also not Western states in the full sense.

This means that the Afro-Asian voting bloc, when it combines with the Soviet bloc, already marshals 35 out of 82 votes, more than the one third necessary to defeat any important resolutions in the General Assembly. When the 14 African states now applying are admitted, the Afro-Asian-Soviet voting strength will be 49 out of 97, or more than half of the General Assembly. The two blocs would then only need to recruit another 14 votes on a particular issue to be able to force through by a two-thirds majority any important resolution, which they liked.

Obviously, this kind of sour calculation need depress us only on issues on which votes divide on bloc lines. But we would be foolish not to recognise that there may be many such issues. Thus, suppose that Panama, inspired by the examples of Cuba and Egypt, decided to use forceful action to gain control of the Panama Canal, analogous to that successfully asserted by Egypt over Suez. And suppose that the US, already threatened by a potential hostile base in Cuba within a hundred miles of the Florida coast, wished to resist Panama's

---

1   Now the Democratic Republic of Madagascar.

demands. Washington would have to face a situation in the United Nations of the following nature.

Security Council action to give United States interests any protection would be barred by the Soviet veto. In the General Assembly, the Afro-Asian and Soviet votes alone would be more than ample to prevent any redress there, and if (as is quite possible) 14 of the 21 Central and South American states sympathised with Panama, there would be enough votes against the United States to carry by a two-thirds majority, recommendations favourable to Panama.

In case we think that this example is far-fetched, it is well to remember that agitation against the American position in the Canal Zone has been increasing in Panama since 1956, and that there were actually riots in the zone early this year.

If the members of the United Nations cannot learn to consider issues on their merits, rather than to gang up in blocs against each other, the organisation will be in danger of breaking up.

There is ground, however, for hoping that they can learn this lesson, as is shown in the Congo resolution of the 17 Afro-Asian states which has just been approved by 70 votes to none in the Emergency Session of the General Assembly, every African state voting for it.

As between the Soviet attempt to censure the Secretary-General and the UN Command for their handling of the UN Congo force, and the view, which I share, that they have handled well an almost impossibly difficult situation, the resolution takes a constructive stand.

It clearly expresses confidence in Mr Hammarskjöld by asking him to continue to carry out the Security Council resolutions, which are his terms of reference in the Congo. It appeals to the Congolese to settle their internal strife peacefully, and calls for contributions to a voluntary UN-controlled fund for economic aid to the Congo. Even more significant, it warns all states to refrain from meddling in the Congo, and bars them from providing military aid except at the request of the United Nations.

Mr Hammarskjöld will therefore not have to carry out his implied threat of resigning, if his actions in the Congo are repudiated. Actually, his immediate position is a very strong one. The UN force was put into the Congo, under his control, by Security Council resolutions in which all the Great Powers concurred. He can only be compelled to withdraw it by another such resolution; and, since the Great Powers are now in disagreement, no such resolution will be forthcoming from the Security Council. Moreover, the Assembly's overwhelming rejection of the Soviet thesis bars any interference through that body.

This does not, of course, mean that the Secretary-General can take the Soviet hostilities lightly. His predecessor, Mr Lie, incurred Soviet hostility because he carried out resolutions that put the United Nations Korean force into the field against communist North Korea. And the Soviet Union waged a three-year campaign of boycott and harassment against him, which finally compelled him to quit the Secretary-Generalship.

Among the thousand demonstrators who gave Cuban leader Fidel Castro a welcome to America, in front of the Shelburne Hotel yesterday, were 700 hysterical women. And among them, the one who really knew what she wanted, was a well-dressed blonde who stretched her arms towards the window at which Castro stood, and cried, 'I don't care what his politics are. He's a real hunk of a man'. Maybe she'd be a good Soviet-sponsored candidate to be the next Secretary-General, if only she has the foresight to pay a similar compliment to the manhood of Mr Khrushchev.

As it was, the march of 2,000 Ukrainian demonstrators which signalled the Soviet Prime Minister's arrival at the East River Pier yesterday was not accompanied by any notes of love and yearning. They screamed and chanted 'Khrushchev the Murderer, Butcher of the Ukraine' and such like abuse, and there were ugly scenes between Polish demonstrators and police, outside the delegation's Park Avenue headquarters. The bobby-sox women outside Fidel Castro's hotel were also later replaced by hostile crowds, and he himself left the hotel after a financial disagreement with the management.

These were not good civic responses to President Eisenhower's appeal to the American people, on the eve of the arrival of nearly a score of heads of state for the Assembly meeting. 'The calm and reasonable conduct of our citizens' the President said, 'will give a renewed demonstration of our nation's sense of responsibility.'

All in all, however, the United States Government acted with correctness in discharging its heavy responsibilities under the UN Headquarters Agreement for the safety of delegates to the General Assembly, and their unimpeded access to the United Nations for the performance of their duties. Before the President's appeal, it was reported that more than 40 anti-Castro groups were planning demonstrations against him; and, but for this appeal and the posting of a record number of police to guard the visitors, their position would have been much more unpleasant.

After all, Mr Khrushchev himself was not exactly a perfect host when, a few months ago, he peremptorily cancelled his invitation to President Eisenhower to visit the Soviet Union, claiming that the Russian people couldn't bear to have him there. No one in Washington invited Mr Khrushchev to come to New York for this General Assembly. As delegates, he and Mr Castro are entitled to physical protection from the American authorities; but they are not really entitled to ask that Americans should make them feel wanted.

PM Menzies Returns After Controversial Speech to General Assembly

Thursday 20 October 1960, Notes on the News, 1.15pm 2BL

Prime Minister Menzies' return home is a proper occasion to reassess the speech, in which he proposed amending the Nehru-Nasser resolution calling for immediate Eisenhower-Khrushchev talks into a less immediate call for a four-power summit meeting in 1961, after the new American President takes office.

Mr Menzies' own story, as he told it at Kingsford Smith airport in Sydney yesterday, and as no doubt he will expand on tonight, contradicted in important respects, the accounts in the Australian press during the course of these last few crazy weeks in the General Assembly.

Mr Menzies says emphatically that the idea of moving this amendment was his own and that he proceeded with it on his own initiative, and he draws attention to its consistency with his previous support of summit conference proposals.

This is, of course, starkly opposed to the picture presented by the press at the time both here and in New York. That picture portrayed Mr Menzies' move as inspired by conversations with Prime Minister Macmillan and President Eisenhower a day or two before; terms of abuse like 'stooge' for Washington policy, 'cat's-paw' of the Western powers, 'fall guy' for Eisenhower and Macmillan, were freely bandied about. Indeed, in the Australian press this line was so dominant that the question of the merits of what Mr Menzies had actually proposed, as compared with what Mr Nehru and co. were proposing, were scarcely considered.

On this point, an article in the *New York Times*, by correspondent Arthur Krock, has now given an interpretation of the events, which supports Mr Menzies' version. Indeed, he presents Mr Menzies as a 'good Samaritan from Down Under', that is, as a man who performed an unrequested and unrequited service because he believed it right. If only Mr Menzies could tell the full story, Krock says, the fire of his Australian critics would have to be turned in other directions than Menzies.

The other point on which Mr Menzies insists, is that he was deeply surprised by Mr Nehru's outburst, in which the Indian Prime Minister bitterly attacked his Australian colleague's proposal and accused him of dealing in trivialities, when he (Nehru) and his four neutralist co-sponsors, in their Eisenhower-Khrushchev tea-for-two resolution, were dealing with grave issues of world importance.

Now this is a very interesting point. As all this was presented to us at the time, Mr Menzies was portrayed, not only as a rather foolish Australian cat's-paw, but as one that was being manipulated in a way that obviously must undermine Australian relations with her Asian neighbours. We were invited to assume, and even told, that this danger to Australian-Asian relations was so obvious that only folly and inexperience in international relations could have led Mr Menzies to do what he did.

No doubt, some Australians who took this critical view of Mr Menzies are his inveterate critics anyhow. But many others were also led to take this view, for at least one reason, which has gone unnoticed. This is a matter of the timetable of the cables from New York. The cables of Nehru's bitter speech came in hard on the heels of those of Menzies' speech itself. By the time we could study what Menzies had said, our attention was jerked away from what he had said, to what Mr Nehru had said.

No, even that isn't right. Our attention wasn't even concentrated on what Mr Nehru had said, but rather on the angry and insulting way in which he had said it. And the inferences were drawn, as if they must be true, first, that Mr Menzies must have taken some anti-Asian line; and second, that Mr Nehru's rather vicious reaction was representative of a justified Asian resentment.

In fact, to construe Mr Menzies' thesis as anti-Asian, you have to take the rather strained view that the reason why he favoured another Big Four Conference was that all the Big Four were of Caucasian rather than mongoloid or African racial stock, that he was drawing a kind of colour line against Asian and African states. But this would be so silly that it could not explain the violent outburst from a man of Mr Nehru's intelligence.

I am afraid I tend to think that the explanation of Mr Nehru's outburst is much simpler. It is a commonplace in all political quarters in India that Jawaharlal Nehru has become, in recent years, increasingly intolerant of all criticism, even when offered from friendly quarters; and increasingly impatient of obstacles to the achievement of whatever objectives he sets for himself. Messrs. Nehru and Nasser, before Mr Menzies' arrival, had taken stances as the head of a small group of five neutralist states; and Mr Nehru's resolution when carried, was to symbolise in Nehru's own mind the consolidation of this power of a neutralist Big Five in the General Assembly under Indian leadership.

From this point of view, and quite regardless of the merits of what either of them proposed, Mr Menzies' intervention seems to have been taken by Mr Nehru as a threat to Indian leadership in the newly organised neutralist cabal. This, rather than any hostility of Asian states generally to anything which Mr Menzies actually said, is a sufficient explanation of Nehru's outburst of anger and impatience. Mr Menzies' amendment to Nehru's resolution was, of course, defeated. But so far, indeed, did Nehru's neutralist Big Five fall short of leading the General Assembly, or even all the Asian nations, that Nehru was compelled shortly afterwards to withdraw the very resolution which he had so angrily defended against amendment by Mr Menzies.

When finally, after departure of the prima donnas, the General Assembly unanimously adopted a resolution calling for immediate steps to solve the 'urgent problems concerning the peace of the world', it was not under neutralist Big Five leadership, but in the usual form of cross-section initiative of 20 members.

It is always a question anyhow what is the significance of talk, or even of resolutions in the General Assembly. But assuming that talk and resolutions are significant, I doubt whether the resolution which Mr Nehru got so excited in defending made as much sense as either Mr Menzies' amendment, or as the resolution finally adopted. No one who knows anything about US politics (and Mr Khrushchev knows plenty) could have expected much good to come from immediate Khrushchev-Eisenhower talks at this stage of the presidential term of office. On the other hand, the building of a basis for a renewed effort for a summit meeting in April or May next year, after the new President of the United States has settled in, makes sense, and so does a call for negotiations on the urgent problems to go ahead in the meantime, on the important level below the so-called summit.

Mr Menzies expressed the view yesterday, on the basis of his 70-minute talk with Mr Khrushchev, that the prospects for a four-power summit conference next year were promising. Incidentally, if Mr Khrushchev had thought that all Asian states were really outraged by Menzies' performance in the General Assembly, he would scarcely have agreed amid so much publicity to this meeting with him, unless, indeed, he had hopes of recruiting Mr Menzies as the leader of a communist satellite state in our part of the world. And even Mr Khrushchev would have blanched at this possibility.

The Crimes Bill and Civil Liberties

Wednesday 23 November 1960, News Commentary, 6.55pm 2BL

After yesterday's rather disgraceful parliamentary session on the Crimes Bill, it is well to remind ourselves of the great issues involved, and try to understand the reasons for the bitterness of this controversy.

No doubt there are many reasons, some accidental, and some personal to Sir Garfield, like his sharp tongue and mind, and his readiness to display these. But the basic reason is in the very nature of the sections dealing with treason, espionage, sabotage and other high offences against the state.

We live in a world in which old-fashioned war between nations has been largely replaced by ambiguous conditions of 'no peace, no war'. And this, together with the relation of ideologies to internal subversion and external threat, accentuates the need for a clear and efficient criminal law.

For these reasons the inclusion in the Crimes Bill of provisions about levying war against 'proclaimed' countries, or assisting the enemies of 'proclaimed' countries, about espionage, sabotage, and official secrets, must be regarded as serious responses to serious challenges, if not of today, then of tomorrow; and not in any mere sinister light.

Sir Garfield and his colleagues regard these problems as so obvious that they hurry to brand critics as either disloyal or the dupes of the disloyal. While many critics with no political or ideological axe to grind, for example critics from the universities and churches, conclude from this attitude that the government is irresponsibly undermining our traditional liberties.

Yet the issues involved should be capable of reasoned instead of angry dialogue. A free people must defend its life and its liberties, and must adjust its defence to the world as it is. But that defence should never, except perhaps momentarily in the very cataclysm of immediate crisis, undermine the very liberties to which it is dedicated.

We could therefore expect, from an Attorney-General who had so admirably steered his bills on telephone tapping and matrimonial causes, the 21 amendments by which he gave guarantees against unnecessary encroachment. These, for instance, removed serious dangers of retrospective punishments for treason and treachery, gave guarantees of bona fide political discussion, criticism and persuasion and of industrial action. It is a pity that Sir Garfield allowed situations to develop which concealed the generosity of these concessions.

He did not, of course, meet all the 40-odd Opposition proposals; and he still did not meet three of my own quite serious criticisms. First, even with the government's concessions, the 'known character' clause still violates basic legal traditions, and places a brooding threat over political free speech and opinion. Second, s.84 still flouts vital principles by allowing arrest and detention without a warrant, and taking away legal redress through the courts for wrongful arrest. Third, s.84(A) (1) (c) commits a similar and I believe unnecessary invasion of liberty.

In a free community the lawyer is in a special sense the watchman of reason in many matters of life and death. No laws come nearer to life and death than those concerning crimes against the state. The Attorney-General, as architect of these laws, holds a supreme watch, where suddenly dangers may loom, but where also shadows from a restless world, or even from a passing cloud, are often mistaken for the assassin's knife. Yet in a free community, an Attorney-General must remain ever the watchman of reason; and he will say, with one of the greatest of judges[1]; 'if we would guide by the light of reason, we must let our minds be bold.'

---

1   Louis Brandeis, Justice of the US Supreme Court 1916–1939.

War in the Congo

Thursday 24 November 1960, Notes on the News, 1.15pm 2BL

The United Nations General Assembly, by a majority of 53 to 24 states with 19 abstentions, has now endorsed the recommendation of its Credentials Committee that the Congo delegation, headed by President Kasa-Vubu, be seated in Assembly, as representing the government of the new state of the Congo.

At that very moment in Léopoldville, capital of the Congo, Congolese troops reputedly of the command of Colonel Mobutu, the strong man behind Kasa-Vubu, and sworn enemy of former Prime Minister Lumumba, were ranged for battle against troops of the United Nations Congo force. The immediate cause of conflict had been the protection afforded by the UN force, of 150 Tunisian soldiers and a squad of Ghanaian police, to the residence of the Ghana Ambassador Welbeck.

Another UN detachment is also guarding the residence in which Mr Lumumba, who still claims to be Premier of the Congo despite his dismissal by President Kasa-Vubu, has been under virtual house arrest for many weeks. And the linkage between the two, according to the Congolese, is that Ghana Ambassador Welbeck has been smuggling 'seditious' documents to Mr Lumumba, is acting generally as his political adviser, and is championing his claim to control the government of the Congo.

As a result, Colonel Mobutu's caretaker College of Commissioners decided to expel the Ghana Ambassador, but that gentleman just slammed the window in the face of the official who conveyed the order to him. Then the fun, or rather the horror, started.

One story is that the Congolese soldiers began shooting at the Ambassador's residence, and UN Tunisian troops returned fire. Another is that Ghana police with the UN force started it. In any case, UN General Rikhye, an Indian, was turned back in his tracks by gunfire, the Congolese commander Colonel Kokola was killed, and there were a number of other deaths and casualties. Afterwards, the Ghana envoy left by plane, still declaring that he was leaving on his own government's instructions, not on the orders of Colonel Mobutu's College of Commissioners.

Meanwhile, on the outskirts of Léopoldville, another Congolese force was threatening an all-out assault on UN Headquarters. And in far off Dublin, seven Irish soldiers, flown home after being killed on UN service in the Congo, were being buried with military honours. They were the first Irish soldiers killed in action since independence, and among the first honoured dead of United Nations forces.

And yesterday through Léopoldville, crowds of 150,000 passed the funeral procession of Colonel Kokola and his other fallen comrades. It was perhaps hopeful that Mr Lumumba joined the mourners' ranks and that some arrested UN officials were released. But it was very unhopeful that UN officials were told to keep away, and that Congolese were menacingly digging in near the home of UN Commander Rikhye.

So when the Soviet delegate who, with the Indian, Ghanaian and Guinean delegates, voted against the seating of President Kasa-Vubu in the General Assembly of the United Nations, they were able to make the plausible point that this was a strange thing to do at a moment when the Congolese soldiers were engaged in virtual battle with the United Nations Force in the Congo. But the strangeness is really only a part of the general strangeness of the whole Congo situation; it may still be the correct thing to do.

Certainly, even if we forget the further complexities and chaos of the provincial and tribal struggles and massacres in Katanga, Kasai, and Orientale, there can rarely have been so tragi-comical and fantastic a diplomatic situation.

It seemed fantastic enough back in August, when the state became formally independent, and everybody started sacking everybody else. Lumumba sacked everyone in sight from Tshombe of Katanga to the Secretary-General. Tshombe ordered the Belgians to stay, and Lumumba and the UN ordered them to go. And then Colonel Mobutu came on to the scene to sack Lumumba and Kasa-Vubu.

But the recent turn of events has even stranger features, and deeper significance. While the Soviet Union and African states like Ghana tried to point to Belgium and other Western countries as the ones intervening in Congo's internal affairs, it turns out to be one of the African states, one of the neutrals supposed to set new standards of non-provocativeness in international conduct, which is the occasion for the first deliberate engagement (as distinct from mere tribal disorder) of UN forces.

There is certainly a moral here, and I don't believe it is the one which Soviet propaganda is trying to draw. It is rather that if you deliberately produce independence for peoples regardless of their readiness, you must expect a period of struggle and chaos before you get any stable order. And you can add to this that if you exclude the big, imperialist nations from meddling, you are likely to find the little, no less imperialist nations meddling, even if they claim to be neutralist.

I am nevertheless still of the view, which I expressed in August, that the attempts through the United Nations Secretary-General and the UN Congo force to hold the Congo ring until the struggle and the chaos subside, is a most important experiment, not least in the down-to-earth experience which it is providing for international officialdom.

But international armies, even if they are only 13,000 strong, still march on their bellies. And Secretary-General Hammarskjöld had to tell the General Assembly that not only were the Congo and the Congo UN force in dire financial straits, but that as a result of the Congo operation the whole United Nations organisation itself was facing the prospect of bankruptcy.

If anything like that happened, of course, the Soviet demand that the UN give up the Congo enterprise, and that the Secretary-General be stripped of his power, would succeed indirectly, where it had failed directly. Moreover, Moscow is well aware of this as a strategy for getting its way both in the Congo, and in the Middle East, where another UN force has played an admirable pacifying role ever since 1956, and continues to do so.

For this problem of financing even small peace forces is a mere continuation of the problem of the Middle East force. And I thought therefore I should dig out for you some figures about the Middle East force.

For the three years 1957–59, the General Assembly levied an assessment on members of $55 million for the Middle East force. By the middle of last year, $20 million of this total was in default. On top of that, an additional $18 million was required for 1960.

Some members therefore were in default, a few of them on the ground that they lacked the means, but clearly the main deficit problem was that nine states, including the entire communist bloc, along with Saudi Arabia, declined any financial responsibility for the peace force. The communist bloc has taken a similar attitude towards the Congo force expenses.

We in Australia are entitled to pride ourselves on the fact that we were one of only three nations (the others were Japan and the Netherlands) who accepted the enlightened view pressed by Mr Hammarskjöld, that the cost of the force should simply be added to the regular budget, so that every member would have to pay his due proportion of it.

This sensible step, however, has never been taken. The Secretary-General, as an emergency measure, began to meet the deficits out of the United Nations capital fund. This has by now been entirely depleted.

Voluntary contributions of members supported the initial stages of the United Nations Congo operations, which cost about $10 million per month. But according to the Secretary-General's report on Tuesday, he needs $20 million by the year's end; otherwise all funds will be exhausted.

The Secretary-General refuted the Soviet charge that he was pursuing in these matters 'a lavish and extravagant spending policy'. And everyone who sincerely desires to see mankind escape from its present muddle, will urge his government to join in that refutation, by answering the plea for financial support for a great enterprise.

Anti-Colonialism; Lumumba Escapes; US Props up UN Finances

Wednesday 30 November 1960, Notes on the News, 1.15pm 2BL

One of the few diplomatic successes which Mr Khrushchev registered during his goings on in New York early in the present General Assembly, was to place on the agenda the so-called 'colonial' issue, which is now being debated in New York.

Even this success was not really major, for the United States has herself taken a steadily anti-colonial line, ever since Roosevelt's time. And despite Mr Churchill's proud declaration during the last war that he had not become the King's first minister to preside at the dissolution of the British Empire, Britain has ever since been giving an ever-accelerating lead in helping her dependent peoples to emancipation. So that the Western states were not concerned so much to stop ventilation of colonial questions, as to prevent these questions being presented in a form that was loaded against them, and in favour of Moscow.

From this point of view, what concerned the United States was not strictly colonies at all, but her own relations with Cuba and other Central and South American states. Dr Castro's marathon speech at the General Assembly, loudly applauded by the Soviet bloc and many Asian states, took the theme that his dispute with Washington arose simply from Washington's imperialist exploitation of Cuba. And he presented his own assaults against US interests as those of a knight in shining armour rescuing Cuba and the Americas from this imperialist dragon.

Despite the headlines at this time, I doubt whether Dr Castro's threats will greatly affect the present discussion of the colonial issue. Virtually all American economic interests in Cuba have by now been seized by Dr Castro, assets running well over a billion dollars. And the United States, by its skilfully timed movement of naval strength into the Caribbean at the request of the Central American states, to prevent the Cuban sponsorship of rebellious incursions against those states, has for the moment sterilised the Cuban plague spot, though leftist rioters in the Venezuelan capital are still shouting Castro-inspired anti-American slogans.

This American success is of great significance, not least because it shows that, despite Moscow's vague threats of using long-range missiles to support Cuba, Washington can and will act to maintain the Monroe Doctrine in the American hemisphere. The fact that there has been no serious reaction from Moscow is significant, however you interpret it – whether you think that the Soviet bluff has been called, or simply sidestepped.

At any rate, the present debate on colonialism is not centred on Cuba, nor is it going quite as Mr Khrushchev planned it. If you read the proceedings hastily you may well indeed wonder quite what has become the issue. The discussion is centred in effect on two rival resolutions and the main line of division is not so much between all Asian and African states, with the communist blocs as their doughty champions. It is rather a division between the communist and a few African and Asian states against the majority of the latter, of whom no less than 28 are sponsoring the rival resolution.

The Soviet-sponsored demand is that colonialism be immediately ended by the grant forthwith of complete independence to all of what Soviet delegate Zorin called the 'hundred million people still languishing in colonial subjugation in the lands of Africa, Asia, Oceania and the Caribbean'.

The rival 28-state Afro-Asian resolution asks only that immediate steps be taken towards ending colonialism where it continues to exist. And since all colonial states (with the exception of Portugal, which is not a UN member) are in any case pledged to bring their dependent peoples to self-government and then to independence at the earliest possible moment, they are not likely to resist the main point of such a resolution.

If this is how it goes, this particular Moscow cracker will also be a bit of a squib. This, indeed, was also indicated by the tenor of the opening discussion. The Soviet design was clear enough. Mr Zorin stigmatised Britain as the foremost colonial power, and accused all colonial powers of plundering colonies, caring for nothing but profit, tolerating high mortality and illiteracy, and racial discrimination, and generally insulting human dignity.

He was answered by the United Kingdom's Ormsby-Gore, who pointed out that since 1939, 500 million people had been helped to independence by Britain, whereas the Soviet record was one of swallowing up peoples formerly independent, not to speak of its satellites, and the coercion exercised to compel its own minorities to submit to Moscow policy. And without intending it, all the communist-bloc states actually proved Mr Ormsby-Gore's point by banging the table in complete unison during his speech, as it were with a single shoe.

But what was even more significant was that the Iranian delegate, who introduced the rival 28-state resolution, made a special point of praising Britain's recent attitudes on colonial issues and the adaptation of her policies to the winds of colonial change. And both he and others deplored attempts to turn the colonial issue into just another issue of the Cold War. And it is notable that the 28-state resolution itself carefully avoids any terms of condemnation of the colonial powers, directing itself wisely to the strategy of the future, rather than recriminations about the past.

The fact is of course, as a prominent Indian diplomat said to me in New Delhi earlier this year, the colonial issue is becoming more and more like the Cheshire cat's grin, without the cat, or the Hamlet drama without the Prince of Denmark. And despite Cold War efforts to the contrary, the Asian nations are becoming increasingly concerned, not about how to force independence, but about what is to happen after independence. And the continuing Congo crisis leads them to think how right they are to do so.

The dismissed Prime Minister Lumumba's escape from house restraint in Léopoldville and the upsurge of support for him in Stanleyville add another complication to a situation which has eased in other aspects since Monday; President Kasa-Vubu, after the seating of his delegation in New York, promised to seek agreement among the contending parties in the Congo, and political talks with President Tshombe of Katanga province, and Kalonji of South Kasai are already arranged. The UN Good Offices committee is due to arrive on 5 December. The enthusiasm of the 100,000 crowd on his return to the capital, the fact that the leading UN officers in the Congo were there to greet him, and that arrested UN personnel have been released, also indicate a great easing of last week's tensions. But all the tough problems are still ahead, and the pro-Lumumba Parliament is still suspended.

Also at UN Headquarters, the financial crisis which threatened the organisation with immediate bankruptcy has been eased, by a most generous US offer, all the more generous because of the present stringency in her overseas payments. But her contribution of 50 percent of the costs still has to be matched by other members undertaking their quotas of financial responsibility. And even then, it will carry the Congo operation only to December. Perhaps we should not ask further what the New Year's resolution of the 99 members will be. Perhaps sufficient unto the year is the Congo thereof.

JFK's Foreign Policy

Thursday 15 December 1960, Notes on the News, 7.15pm 2BL

A main argument used by Mr Nixon's supporters against President-elect Kennedy was that he was young and inexperienced, an argument most telling in relation to foreign policy. And thousands of intelligent folk throughout Asia and Africa have been asking, since his election, what difference his administration will make to the many grave issues of the world crisis.

Not that Mr Kennedy had not formulated reasonably clear positions on many of these issues, even long before the rather footling and indecisive exchanges during the election campaign.

Whether in Senate speeches or in his 1959 book, *The Strategy of Peace*, Kennedy had committed himself on most of these issues. On some of them his position was rather indistinguishable from the Dulles-Eisenhower-Herter line. Like them, for example, he was determined to defend Berlin, if necessary by nuclear war. 'If you are driven from Berlin', he said on 1 August 1959, 'you are driven from Germany, from Europe, from Asia and Africa and then our time will come next.' Nor was there any clear departure in his views of German unity, or of the impracticability of dramatic action for the liberation of Soviet satellites in Eastern Europe. He accepted the Soviet military reaction to the Hungarian revolt (as did the Eisenhower Administration) as limiting the possibility of US action to encouraging any discontent by modest measures of cultural exchanges and economic aid.

Even his much publicised dispute with Nixon over the Chinese offshore islands boiled down to very little. He charged Nixon with being ready to plunge America into war for a few useless islands; and Nixon charged him with saying that their defence was not worth the bones of a single American soldier. But by the time they had come to grips, it was clear that they were both agreed that the islands were not worth defending for their own sake; but that they emphatically must be defended from any Chinese attack which was really aimed at Chiang Kai-shek's Nationalist Chinese government on Formosa (Taipei). And the argument petered out with Nixon's rather Gilbertian proposition (when uttered to millions of TV listeners) that his real point was that they should not tell Communist China what their intentions were as to Matsu and Quemoy.

Even as regards Washington's relations with Peking, the difference was only a matter of degree. Kennedy would continue to oppose recognition and admission to the United

Nations. But he always carefully put in the word 'now' and stressed the importance of improving communication with mainland China. And the only difference in relation to summit conferences is that Mr Khrushchev has graciously let it be known that he does not regard Kennedy as tainted with U2 spy plane guilt.

If I had to pick the points on which Kennedy's pronouncements clearly promised a change of foreign policy, they would be mainly four.

As to defence budgeting, he is committed, without any sops to taxpayers, to spend just as much as is necessary to produce what he calls a 'nuclear retaliatory power second to none', a phrase which he repeated yesterday in announcing the appointment as Defence Secretary of Robert McNamara, the president of the giant Ford Motor Company. There is much speculation as to what degree of shake-up and reorganisation of the Pentagon is involved, and it is impossible to draw any reliable clues on this from McNamara's appointment. After all, Mr Eisenhower's Defence Secretary was Charles E. Wilson, the president of the General Motors Corporation. While Ford and General Motors are sharp competitors, the men who get to the top of both are not likely to be too different from each other, even though McNamara is known as rather an intellectual, and Wilson was known as 'Engine Charlie'.

Second, conversely to this plank for nuclear preparedness, Kennedy has stressed that not all defence eggs should be put into the nuclear basket. Nuclear weapons cannot be used to meet minor threats, such as the crisis in Laos or the Congo, however aggressive. Kennedy is pledged to regain what he calls 'the ability to intervene effectively and swiftly in any limited war'.

The third difference, and the most important of all, is undoubtedly in the matter of foreign aid. Many economists and other commentators have urged for years now that Western economic aid to underdeveloped countries cannot yield its full benefits, whether economic or political, as long as it is uncertain what appropriations Congress is going to give from year to year. Kennedy is pledged to increase the flow of such aid on a basis that will permit long-term commitment.

And when he speaks in this connection of Asia, Africa, the Middle East and Latin America, it is clear that Kennedy gives a central place to India. And he has put his motives quite bluntly. 'It is vital,' he said in June last 'that we aid India to make a success of her new five-year program – a success that will enable her to compete with Red China for economic leadership of all Asia'.

This is the background, I think, against which we will most appreciate two other key appointments which Mr Kennedy has just announced, Chester Bowles as Assistant Secretary of State, with Dean Rusk of the Rockefeller Foundation as Secretary of State.

Despite the fact that my recent visit to India was in the recent after-glow of President Eisenhower's visit, the American diplomat whose memory I found warmest and freshest among my Indian friends was that of Chester Bowles, the first United States Ambassador to independent India. Both then and in his later books, he has made the rapid progress and stability of India a first plank of American foreign policy.

Kennedy not only adopted this plank in his electioneering; the Bowles appointment seems a step to implement it.

Dean Rusk's appointment as Secretary of State, when you know his background, points in a similar direction. Dean Rusk has been for nearly ten years' head of the Rockefeller Foundation, after earlier experience in government as assistant to the Secretary of War, and then at the desk of Far Eastern Affairs in the State Department.

But I think it may help to take a glimpse of what the Rockefeller Foundation is at present doing. Picking at random from a hundred activities mentioned in the last Annual Report of the foundation, I see that the foundation's overseas program embraces Virus Research Centres in Poona,[1] and on the Madras coastal plain in India; an Indian Agricultural Program; a Mexican Agricultural Program concentrating on the effects of diverse crops on fertility; projects on corn, wheat and beans in Colombia, and on pasture enrichment in Chile, and on the reclamation of millennially neglected land in the Israeli Negev. And I should not have to remind Australian listeners that it is the Rockefeller Foundation that has made possible the great 210-foot radio telescope at Parkes, in New South Wales, under the direction of the CSIRO.

It is thus a fair inference that Kennedy chose Dean Rusk and Chester Bowles with an eye focused on foreign economic aid. Adlai Stevenson as Secretary of State would obviously have had a wider range, including high strategy and policy. He is to be Ambassador to the United Nations, where his ideas will no doubt have ample play, but where he will not be in a position either to dominate the State Department, or to inhibit the style of the youngest President by his seniority in politics.

The President's team for foreign policy, then, probably includes the best talent the President could find in his party, even though not quite in the positions that use the talents best.

The stringency in American overseas funds may, of course, baulk the good intentions of the Kennedy team. And the new transatlantic Organisation for Economic Organisation and Development, just announced from Paris, is designed to bring the other 19 prosperous Western states into a joint enterprise of economic aid to underdeveloped people.

---

1   Pune, India

End of Decade Reflections

Friday December 30, 1960, Notes on the News, 1.15pm

Though I shall be speaking to you next Tuesday night in the fourth ABC lecture, this is my last opportunity to wish you all a Happy New Year before 1961 is actually ushered in.

Having said this, I feel I want to go on and tell you something of what we must envisage as our common future as we wish each other a Happy New Year.

Of course, if I were expressing my wishes out of the context of our actual world in this our century, I would envisage for us all a year in which, besides your own personal health and happiness and prosperity, all anxieties concerning the possibilities of war, and all the day-to-day tension and irritation of international relations become a thing of the past – a barely remembered nightmare.

I would envisage that Moscow and Washington would turn their tremendous resources and their marvellous skills and energy into the common program for developing the peaceful use of atomic energy which they have been talking about for years. Instead of these nations extending the Cold War into outer space, I would envisage the epic heroism of man's entry into this vast and exciting new inheritance under their joint leadership.

But for the context of our world and century, too, my wishes could envisage that 1961 could bring to peoples everywhere an emancipation from poverty and ignorance and disease which still particularly affect a thousand million of our fellow men in the backward countries of Asia; and that the hates and fears and violence which we and they inherit from a colonial era already past could be transmuted quickly into human kindness and helpfulness.

For this emancipation from poverty, ignorance and disease is far more crucial for the human future, and far more difficult to achieve, than the political emancipation of the few remaining colonial areas. What a difference it could make to the economic advancement of the poorer countries, and to the spiritual development of the richer ones, if even a small proportion of the energy and treasure spent on weapons could be dedicated to the humanity-wide campaign against poverty, ignorance and disease.

These and many other wonderful things I could envisage if my wishes for 1961 did not have to be offered in the context of the actual world.

Already, indeed, the potentialities are there this last week of 1960. A new era in man's control over his environment has opened within the US satellite Tiros II transmitting clear pictures on a continental scale of cloud formations above the earth from its regular 100-minute orbit course around the earth. The new American President's advisers have just announced a great speed-up of the US space program, and the Soviet Union is said to be on the verge of a manned flight into space and back.

A loan just announced of nearly £122 million mainly from the United States and the International Monetary Fund will enable Yugoslavia to overhaul its foreign exchange and trade systems; and the United States will provide Formosa with the means to carry out a vast power, irrigation and flood control plan in Formosa, including the construction of one of the world's highest dams. And it is part of Kennedy's election platform to expand US economic aid to underdeveloped areas, and place aid on long-term international bases to allow long-term planning by the assisted countries.

But these things are still only potential, and cannot be envisaged except as long-term objectives. In the shorter run what we have to envisage is not the disappearance of the grave anxieties of the decade which 1960 closes, but only that our anxieties do no become more acute, and above all, do not prove justified by the outbreak of large-scale violence.

For this last week of 1960 has been marked also by too many ominous signs. In the Congo the civil war is still building up, and the 100 members of the General Assembly adjourned that session in verbal deadlock as to what instructions to give the Secretary-General and the UN force. Belgium was threatened with a general strike, and even civil strife, over trade union resistance to the austerity measures designed to adjust the economy to the loss of the Congo economy. The Belgian crisis paralleled the chronic crisis which still baffles France's relations with Algeria.

With the military success over the leftists of the pro-Western government in Laos, Peking and Moscow were threatening that general war might spring from the Laos civil war. Washington, Moscow and Peking were becoming increasingly open in supplying military aid to their favoured sides, and on Wednesday a Soviet transport plane shot at a US plane which was observing the Soviet air-drop of supplies to left-wing forces in Laos.

In the troubled belt which stretches to our own shores, the Indonesian government set itself this week on a course rather inconsistent with its repeated undertaking not to resort to force in pressing its claim to Dutch New Guinea. It sent to Moscow a mission to purchase heavy arms, and openly stated that the arms it now sought were for external action against Dutch forces in New Guinea, to supplement the small arms for internal security which it gets from the United States.

And further to our East, in the Pacific, 1,000 miles north of Fiji, a Soviet submarine was thought to be testing a Polaris-type of missile, fired from under water.

The 2,000-mile frontier between India and Communist China remains as active as ever as 1961 opens. And in New Delhi itself, the Indian government claimed yesterday to have broken three spy rings, each of them having in its pay employees of the Indian Ministries of Defence and External Affairs – about eight of whom have been arrested. It is characteristic of this Mecca of neutralism that the three spy rings are thought to have been operated by one communist, and one Western, and one neighbouring state – presumably Communist China.

And so we could go on. France chose this last week to explode her third nuclear device in the Sahara, producing hostile comments from the communist world, and from most of the new African states, who are preparing for a conference to discuss the problems of the continent from French Algeria to South African apartheid, early in the New Year. And Mr

Khrushchev chose this moment for renewing his political warfare on the rather phoney issues of the ending of colonialism and reform of the United Nations.

But the point I am making is clear enough. My wishes to you for 1961 are as sincere as they can be; but they should not give you false hopes of any sudden change for the better in the general international outlook. Does this mean that general war is more likely? That is a different question; and my answer to it is that it is neither more likely nor less likely than in 1960.

In late 1949 I remember telling my listeners that I did not share the then current war panic following the Berlin Blockade and our awareness of Soviet atomic know-how. My view was that if both sides could manage to get through the decade without a major war, the chances of long-term survival would be very good. When there is no quick and clean way of removing tension, peoples, like individuals, either crack under the strain or learn to live with them.

On balance, the events of 1950–60 seem to me to show that this was not too far wrong. Is it still so for 1961? I think it is, with two qualifications – one good, one bad.

The good one is that we can be much more confident now, than in 1950, that the peoples of the world can stand this amount of tension without cracking and learn to live with it; the ten years just past have been a fair test of this capacity.

The bad thing is that, at a time when Moscow and Washington are still far from agreement about control of nuclear weapons, other new powers, including France and probably Communist China, are making moves to enter the club, and we may be approaching a stage of simpler and cheaper bombs within the reach of other small nations. This development would, as C.P. Snow said yesterday, greatly increase the danger of these weapons being used. And if Washington and Moscow were at loggerheads on everything else in the world, they would still have a vital common interest in preventing an indiscriminate distribution of atomic striking power.

The Origins of SEATO's Refusal to Intervene in Laos

Thursday 5 January 1961, News Commentary

Today's cables from Washington, from the Laotian capital and from the SEATO Council meeting at Bangkok, focus attention on the possible functions of SEATO in relation to the struggle between the pro-Western Laos government of Prince Boun Oum and pro-communist Pathet Lao.

From Washington, India and Britain are reported to favour the return to Laos of the neutral Control Commission (with India, Poland and Canada as members), established by the Geneva Conference in 1955, but later ousted by the Laotian government. US opposition is said to be softening.

From Vientiane, pro-Western government Defence Minister Nosavan is reported to be expressing hopes of an early peaceful settlement with the Pathet Lao, but there are conflicting reports as to the attitude towards return of the International Commission.

More significant is Nosavan's clear statement that this government is not seeking military help from SEATO and would not do so except in case of a large-scale foreign invasion of Laos.

This item is to be linked with the SEATO Council report that no such invasion has been proved, and that the majority favour a political settlement by broadening the pro-Western government to include some Pathet Lao elements, and want Laos to take a neutral position in the Cold War. When so linked, it adds up, despite provocative Soviet aid to Pathet Lao, to a political rather than a military showdown.

Some people may be wondering why SEATO seems to dither so much about military action in Laos. But a glance at the history and constitution of SEATO gives a clear enough answer.

Historically, from its birth, SEATO was suspended between two radically different theses. For Washington put in an express reservation focused on military action against communist aggression. But for London and most Asian members, SEATO was rather to be a political Locarno-type arrangement to assure stability by compromise, rather than fighting it out in southwest Asia. Its work was to supplement the results of the General Conference. Fully developed in this conception, SEATO would have embraced neutralist states like India, and possibly even communist states. But it never did.

You will readily see that the recent attitudes of London, Washington and New Delhi, about what to do in Laos, continue the conflicting conceptions which begat SEATO.

Constitutionally, the reason for the lack of military drive in SEATO is no less clear. While the United States wanted the treaty to cover communist aggression over the whole of east and south Asia, the 'treaty area' finally fixed was much more limited. Its northern limits were at 21 degrees 30 minutes of latitude, leaving Formosa and Korea beyond. And it was further provided that, even south of this line, military action should not be taken in the Indochinese states, including Laos, without the consent of the governments of those countries.

The fact that even the present pro-Western government of Laos declares that it needs no military help, therefore, would block SEATO intervention even if a majority of the SEATO Council members favoured it, which they do not.

The Secretary-General of SEATO is reported to have said today that SEATO cannot act in Laos until invasion by foreign communist forces is confirmed. This is true, so far as the SEATO pact is aimed against international aggression and not at civil war within a state. But if taken out of context, this is a misleading half-truth, implying as it does, that if there were such a foreign invasion, SEATO could and would take military action. For such action could not, even then, take place without the consent of the government of Laos. The present pro-Western government, as we have seen, still gives a polite 'no'; any broadened government succeeding the present one would be likely to be less polite, but still say no.

Is SEATO Worth Its Price?

Sunday 15 January 1961, Australia and the World, 2BL

From the very signing of the Manila Treaty on 8 September 1954 – officially known as the Southeast Asia Collective Defence Treaty – those responsible, and especially the late Mr Dulles, gave a warning against calling it SEATO.

That warning was against thinking of the new organisation as a Southeast Asian counterpart of NATO – that is, as a military organisation equipped with standing forces contributed by the members, with a joint command standing ready to repel any military attack on a member. And when, later on, the question arose whether there should be a military headquarters of SEATO based on Singapore, as the British wished, no agreement was reached. All this has meant, in effect, that the great United States base at Manila remains the source of any military power of SEATO. While Mr Dulles spoke of SEATO having a mobile striking force rather than a standing military establishment, the reality rather is that, if SEATO wishes and if the United States wishes, the United States will place mobile striking power at SEATO's disposal.

The absence of any joint command structure, analogous to that of NATO, has been mitigated only by a degree of military planning co-operation between the members, and by a series of joint training exercises in land warfare, landing operations and joint air-ground staff work, mainly involving Thailand and the United States.

It is somewhat paradoxical that the United States, which has been lukewarm from the start about making SEATO an independent military factor for defending Southeast Asia, should also reputedly have been the member which, in crises like the present one in Laos, as well as the earlier crisis at Dien Bien Phu, has had to be dissuaded from seeking military solutions. But perhaps this is not so strange after all. Washington is no doubt conscious that it is the decisive military force in the area. If there is an independent source of military decision in SEATO, which has forces to deploy, this would limit its own freedom of decision in a crisis. In short, the modesty of the American conception of SEATO as a military instrument, reflects the high importance which Washington attaches to having her own hands free to use her own military power.

This gives us an important clue also to some of the main conflicts between London and Washington as to the overall role that SEATO should play in south and southeast Asia. Broadly, Washington has seen SEATO as a support for its own military effort to contain the expansion of communism in this area, as providing its Asian members with bases of military operation, if need be, against Chinese communist or Soviet advances towards the ocean in Southeast Asia, and therefore as continental advance posts of the strategic chain of islands from the Aleutian Islands to the Philippines on which its Pacific naval power is based.

The United Kingdom, on the other hand, hoped that SEATO could be an instrument for pacification of the area through diplomatic compromise, a meeting ground between the western states and not only their pro-Western Asian friends, like the Philippines, Thailand and Pakistan, but also neutralist Asian states like India and (at moments) even communist-sympathising states such as North Vietnam and Indonesia.

The story of SEATO since 1954 represents an indecisive struggle between these different conceptions of its goals; and this struggle has set the pattern of developments in the present long drawn out crisis in Laos. Until the crisis broke, American influence in Laos was unchallenged and the pro-Western government steadily cast off the ties of the compromise reached at the Geneva Conference, and ousted the International Supervisory Commission of Indian, Canadian and Polish membership set up at Geneva.

The neutralist Laotian government, pledged to co-operate with the leftist Pathet Lao, which emerged in the first phase of the current struggle, was recognised by Moscow and Peking, but was overthrown at least temporarily by a restored pro-Western government, of course recognised by the West. The last few weeks have seen a regular seesaw between the two conflicting views in the Western camp. The Washington view is that the only answer to communist activity is to increase military aid to the pro-Western forces and even intervene directly to repel forces allegedly invading Laos from communist North Vietnam. Late this week it was reported that the US had delivered four armed observation planes and a number of helicopters to the pro-Western government, allegedly because Russia had troops fighting with communist forces in central Laos, and was still dropping supplies to the pro-communist forces.

The United Kingdom's view, on the other hand, was that what was called for was a broadening of the pro-Western government by representation in it of pro-communist elements of Pathet Lao, yielding a more stable government, but one more neutralist as between the Western and communist worlds.

Last week, it was reported that the majority of the SEATO Council, consisting of Australia France, New Zealand, Pakistan, the Philippines, Thailand, the United Kingdom and the United States, favoured the British kind of response, and that the pro-Western Lao government was agreeable to a broadened representation, and possibly to the return of the International Supervisory Commission, and had declared that it did not need direct military intervention by SEATO on its behalf.

The latest move now under consideration in the Western capitals is a proposal by the head of the neighbouring state of Cambodia, Prince Norodom Sihanouk, that there should be a diplomatic conference of the 14 states, which are immediately involved, one way or another, in the Laotian fracas. Of these 14, eight would consist of the parties to the Geneva Agreement of 1954, namely France, the United Kingdom, the United States, Russia, North Vietnam, Communist China, Cambodia, and Laos, three would be the states represented on the International Advisory Commission, namely India, Poland and Canada, and the other three would be the neighbouring states of Thailand, South Vietnam and Burma. Russia, France, Britain, and North Vietnam are reported as favourable to the proposal, and the United States has hedged on the proposal rather than reject it.

The pointers, therefore, are to a diplomatic compromise rather than a military showdown, unless there is some dramatic new military development in the internal civil war. From the official Washington standpoint, this is likely to increase the doubts as to the value of SEATO as a bastion against communist aggression, and subversion in Southeast Asia. From the British point of view, it will be evidence that SEATO is a useful brake and guide on political development in this area.

And, to be fair, I should also make it clear that there is an important and informed body of American opinion which has become articulate in the last year or so, which is extremely critical of the official Washington concept of SEATO as a part of the American system of military defence.

In an important article in January 1960, the editor of the American quarterly *Foreign Affairs*, Hamilton Fish Armstrong, points out that as an instrument of military policy SEATO has several basic weaknesses. First, only three states of the region – the Philippines, Thailand and (with a big stretch) Pakistan, are members of it, while India, Ceylon, Burma and Indonesia have been hostile from the start. Even Malaya, which was one of the main areas that SEATO was designed to protect, stayed out when it became independent.

Second, this not only means that little military strength comes from the Asian members; it also means that the non-members have tended to regard SEATO as a Western colonialist conspiracy directed against the new Asian states. Third, at least two of the Asian members of SEATO have chronic and bitter disputes with neighbouring states, Pakistan with India and Afghanistan, and Thailand with Cambodia and South Vietnam. These neighbouring states look with particular suspicion and resentment at any military or political support provided by SEATO to its Asian members. And the Western members are charged with upsetting the military balance in the region, and the effect is not only that Western relations with Asia are not improved by SEATO, but that they are positively undermined, and the aggrieved Asian states are pushed towards Moscow and Peking.

This minority American view leads to the conclusion that Washington should give up the idea that SEATO can be an effective instrument of military defence, and that American policy should proceed on the basis that Washington should seek to make all the states of the region its friends, without asking any of them to be its allies. No military effectiveness would be sacrificed by this since, then as now, America would stand ready to help victims of aggression who asked for it; which is all that it can do at the moment, as the Laotian situation shows.

Instead of a SEATO including only a small rump of pro-Western Asian states, efforts should be made to promote a mutual defence organisation consisting of the Asian states, which would be free, if it wished, to call for Western aid in any emergency. There is, of course no immediate prospect of this kind of development; but three long-term factors make it worth speculating on. In the first place, Indian fear and disillusionment with Peking over communist encroachment on its northern frontiers are shared more or less by other Asian states. Secondly, it is a main objective of Ayub Khan's revolutionary regime in Pakistan to settle his country's major differences with India, not only about the Indus waters on which a successful outcome is already assured, but also in Kashmir. Third, the time must be approaching when India herself will recognise that either Peking or New Delhi must provide leadership in south and southeast Asia. If her third Five Year Plan succeeds and Nehru is spared for sufficient years, India may squarely meet this challenge; and a mutual defence system with her Asian neighbours would be a fine arena for her leadership.

Kennedy's Inauguration; Australia's Universities; Khrushchev – Communism Does Not Need War

Friday 30 January 1961, Notes on the News, 1.15pm 2BL

The inauguration of incoming President Kennedy will take place with great pomp and circumstance.

When the oath is administered to the new President, however, there will not be the grim solemnity and the desperate anxiety, which marked the inauguration of Democrat Franklin D. Roosevelt nearly 30 years ago, when the stock market had collapsed, and the wheels of industry groaned and had squealed almost to a stop amid the debris, while the nation's banks had clanged their doors shut against their customers.

But while the grimness and the desperation will be less, solemnity and anxiety there will be aplenty in the mind and heart of this youngest of presidents and among all thoughtful Americans. Whatever departures from Eisenhower's policies Kennedy may initiate, he certainly shares many of the forebodings expressed on Tuesday by the outgoing President.

One of these concerned 'the temptation to feel that some spectacular and costly action could become the miraculous solution of all current difficulties'. The incoming president, who takes an even dourer view of American foreign policy, knows that he must learn to endure this long continuing crisis, and to teach his people to endure it, without either yielding, or provoking a military showdown.

Another foreboding of Mr Eisenhower concerned the danger of increasing concentration of power in the hands of the military and the technologists and scientists, as national defence comes increasingly to rest on the combination between these groups – the 'complex', as he called it – of military and scientific technological elites. 'We must never' he said, 'let the weight of this combination endanger our liberty or democratic processes'.

Still another foreboding of Mr Eisenhower concerned the effect of these same developments on American university life. Because of the massive finance required by modern scientific research, and because most research becomes increasingly tied in with government policy and projects, defence and otherwise, universities are in danger of becoming mere tools of the political authority.

Even in this country the federal government's contribution to universities in 1960–61 reached £11 million; yet this will prove, I am sure, disastrously inadequate.

The question which President Eisenhower was raising – and we might recall that he came to the presidency of the United States from the presidency of the great Columbia University – could be formulated thus. Today more than ever, the standing of his nation, and ours too, depends on developing to their fully extended limits the intellectual resources and potentialities of each generation. This requires far more than acceptance by each scholar of the existing body of knowledge. It requires, more than ever before, adventure and daring by individual scholars and free communication and co-operation between them.

It requires, in short, that universities, as communities of scholars, should maintain their intellectual independence, integrity and initiative, especially as against government and its demands. How are universities to do this, when they are so abjectly and increasingly dependent on generous governmental subsidies?

Clearly, they cannot do it unless most citizens insist that universities should be assured of both the independence and the money necessary to their role as the intellectual power house of the nation; and also unless the executive government and parliament remain responsible to the people.

It is precisely in this context that President Eisenhower warned of the great danger, under modern defence conditions, that real power may slip into the hands of the military and the technologists, even when they do not seek it.

This is a lesson, which we in Australia should heed even at this stage. £11 million for our main teaching universities seems a big sum of federal money, if you don't know from the inside, the magnitude of the demands on universities, and if you forget that, after all, you are dealing with the national investment in the basic education and training of our best intellectual resources. Unless this task is well done in each generation, all aspects of our national life, including our economic stability, and defence planning, will falter and break down.

Yet this total federal contribution to all Australian universities outside Canberra is actually less than what the government is spending on just two of its own technological agencies. The federal Commonwealth Scientific, Industrial and Research Organisation (CSIRO) and the Atomic Energy Commission will receive this year more than £12½ million.

Now these government agencies perform indispensable tasks. The money they spend is as well spent as public money can be. But that is not the point: the point is rather that unless universities are also enabled financially to educate each generation to an adequate level, technological agencies of this sort will fold up in the not so long run. This thought underlines the complaint yesterday of Dr W. Boas, a division chief of the CSIRO, that it is 'completely wrong' that scholars should have to promise quick practical discoveries before they can get funds for research.

To take adequate care of our technological agencies because the usefulness of their work is easier to see, while penny-pinching on the needs of universities, is short-sighted folly. What would we think of an industrialist who equipped his factory with wonderful modern machinery but failed to attend to the adequacy of the system by which power is produced and fed to his plant?

Mr Khrushchev's interpretation on Wednesday of the declaration of last November's Conference of Communist Parties in Moscow, provides a convenient commentary on Eisenhower's warning against expecting any quick solution to the international crisis. Mr Khrushchev blandly tells us that communism does not need war to take over the world, though it may have to use arms if capitalism resists. This presumably means – charitably interpreted – that communism will only use arms if Western states resist, by force, the victory of communism through peaceful competition.

But it is difficult to indulge this charitable interpretation when Mr Khrushchev simultaneously confirms communist support for all so-called 'wars of national liberation', and the Soviet policy of unilaterally threatening to use thermo-nuclear weapons under the pretext of 'snuffing out' brush fire wars.

'Wars of Liberation', and snuffing out brush fire wars, are high-sounding objectives which seem as if all peoples should share them. But as long as Moscow interprets them any way it pleases, they can also be mere hypocritical slogans of Soviet political warfare, covers for using force or the threat of force without the risk of receiving blow for blow. It is a tactic which, coming from Mr Khrushchev, I might call, if you will forgive the quip, coercion by buffoonery. The gravest problem of American foreign policy is to steer a course towards fruitful negotiation between the rocks, on the one hand, of credulous submission to such coercion by buffoonery, and, on the other, impetuous reaction to it by a resort to force.

Attack on the Secretary-General

Monday 20 February 1961, Notes on the News, 1.15pm 2BL

The national delegations to the United Nations in New York spent much of the weekend contemplating three developments in the Congo crisis.

One is the Soviet resolution tabled immediately after the announcement of Mr Lumumba's death, demanding the dismissal of Secretary-General Hammarskjöld, the withdrawal of United Nations forces from the Congo, and the imposition of sanctions against Belgium on the theory of her responsibility, presumably through her influence in Katanga Province, for Mr Lumumba's death.

Another is the report of the Advisory Committee on the Congo appointed early in the Congo affair, but which remained in enforced inactivity until December, when it went to the Congo, ostensibly to promote a conference of the various factional leaders.

The committee's plan for a meeting at that time was frustrated by the series of events associated with Mr Lumumba's escapes and recaptures, events which culminated last week in his announced death at the hands of Katanga villagers, allegedly (according to the Tshombe Katanga version) in the course of an attempt to escape.

After six weeks in the Congo, the committee has obviously not had many brainwaves. The so-called summit conference of Congo leaders, which it proposes, is no different from what it was proposing when it arrived in the Congo (except that Mr Lumumba is now dead, and the place of meeting now proposed is outside the Congo). It also thinks, despite some members who were Lumumba supporters, that federalism is the only possible basis for Congolese unity. This recommendation too was all but explicit in the situation as it was when the committee originally left New York.

At that time, the Kasa-Vubu delegation had won recognition as representing the legitimate government of the Congo, over the claims of the Lumumba faction. It is important to remember, at this stage, that from the start Lumumba and his party have stood for a centralised government of the Congo, whereas the anti-Lumumba forces have opposed centralisation from two rather different standpoints. One is that of the strong tribal organisation, which is still the basis of Congolese life, and with which President Kasa-Vubu is closely associated. The other is the secessionist trend in Katanga Province where the main wealth of the Congo – copper – is concentrated, and in South Kasai, where most of the rest of the wealth lies, in the form of 80 percent of the world's industrial diamonds.

So that when the UN Conciliation Commission now recommends the federal principle as a basis for compromise between the factions, it is proposing a settlement largely on the basis of the status quo. And Lumumba's successor, Mr Gizenga, if given a place in a new coalition government, will have to come in essentially on those terms. And those terms will almost certainly be acceptable to the great Belgian corporations of Forminière and Union Minière, whose concessions in Katanga and South Kasai run for another 30 years.

The other main recommendations of the Conciliation Committee are that the UN Congo force should remain in charge of peace and order, and that the army controlled by strong man Mobutu, who stands behind President Kasa-Vubu, should be insulated from all political activity. Exactly how either of these miracles is to be achieved, with a UN force of only 17,000 men (including the additional Malayan contingent just announced) is not yet very clear. Remember that the Congo Republic is bigger than India, and 11 times bigger than Britain.

I am saying, in short, that there is little prospect that the Conciliation Committee's report will produce any serious change inside the Congo, though it may help to stabilise the Kasa-Vubu regime by its endorsement of the federalist principle.

The greater dangers for the Congo situation arise, in my opinion rather from international developments in New York, than from internal forces. Besides the Soviet resolution already mentioned, two others will be before the Security Council after it resumes its deliberations today.

One is an Afro-Asian resolution authorising use of the UN force to prevent full-scale civil war. This draft resolution is a great encouragement to the Secretary-General, who had declared in reply to the Soviet attack that he placed his future in the hands of the uncommitted nations, and would neither resign nor yield to the Soviet boycott, unless those nations told him to. Their answer is to offer him more authority.

According to the latest cable, Prime Minister Nkrumah of Ghana is to go to New York with yet another plan for placing control of the Congo under an all-African command, disarming all Congolese factions, and removing all foreign embassies. Whatever else this means, it also does not endorse Soviet strong-arm methods against the Secretary-General. Only three delegations, in fact, Guinea, Mali and Cuba, have spoken in favour of it and against Mr Hammarskjöld.

As the Soviet spaceship moves towards Venus, we should keep a sense of proportion about Soviet infallibility. From the vehemence of its demands for UN reorganisation, many in the West have assumed that Moscow again has the West on the defensive.

I do not take that view. I think, on the contrary, that Moscow regards itself as having blundered in ever agreeing to the Security Council resolution putting the UN force into the Congo. No doubt, at the time, Moscow thought that the force was bound to be a thorn in the flesh of Belgian interests in the Congo, and that it could not prejudice Soviet interests.

When things turned out otherwise, and the Congo government sheered away from her, Moscow was faced with the hard fact that she could not get the Congo force out without a Security Council vote, on which the Western states each could have a veto.

I believe the attack on Mr Hammarskjöld is merely an attempt to get, indirectly, a withdrawal of UN forces which Moscow cannot get directly by Security Council resolution.

I believe that this is the deeper meaning of the parallel between the Soviet attack on Trygve Lie over the Korean affair from 1950 onwards, and the present attack on Hammarskjöld, for in Korea in 1950 she also blundered.

The Soviet blunder over Korea in 1950 was that she was boycotting the Security Council meetings which adopted the first Korea resolutions.

The important question, then, is not whether Moscow may be able to freeze Hammarskjöld out of his job before his term expires in 1963. It is whether he can be pushed out in conditions which do not permit any substitute UN leadership in the Congo, and before that country gets onto an even keel.

Africa Withdraws from the Commonwealth

Monday 20 March 1961, Notes on the News, 1.15pm 2BL

When the South African Prime Minister gets back to home base, after serving notice that the republic, shortly to be born, will not be a member of the Commonwealth, he will be confronted by three streams of political thought.

In his own Nationalist Party, with its solid Afrikaner membership, there will be fanatical praise for what they regard as his double achievement. First, in the recent referendum the Prime Minister led his white countrymen out of the allegiance to the British Crown to the status of a republic. By this, rather paradoxically, he ranged his country among the coloured, rather than the white communities of the Commonwealth, with India and Pakistan and Ghana, which are republics, rather than with Australia, New Zealand and Canada.

Second, they believe that, by the quiet bombshell which Prime Minister Verwoerd dropped last week when he withdrew the request of his Republic of South Africa for Commonwealth membership, he had taken a stand, despite enormous pressure, which will save South Africa from becoming dominated by black voters, with white people, both Afrikaans and English, a minority legally and politically at their mercy.

On this basis, all Afrikaners and their organisations will try to make the Prime Minister's return a triumphal occasion.

But whether this stream of political thought is more than a short-sighted self-delusion may not really be within the Prime Minister's power to decide.

It will be decided rather by the strength of another movement, for which the voice this week was that of native leader of the outlawed African Congress, Chief Luthuli. Luthuli has always been a moderate African leader, favouring a co-operative common society of white and black. On hearing the news of South Africa's break with the Commonwealth, he declared that it led him to rejoice, for he saw it as a blow against South Africa's apartheid policies.

And, in the spirit of Luthuli, it is reported that the outlawed parties have sent a call for anti-apartheid demonstrations to coincide with the return of Dr Verwoerd, and the anniversary of last year's tragedy in Sharpeville.

So these two strains of political thought and movement will confront each other this week at high tension, one triumphantly convinced that South Africa is now committed once and for all to apartheid, and that her fate lies in the hands of the white minority; the other triumphantly convinced that the pressure of Commonwealth opinion that compelled South Africa to abandon her membership is now committed solidly against apartheid, and that an isolated South Africa outside the Commonwealth cannot in the long run resist this pressure.

Between the two stands the non-Afrikaner and English-speaking white population of South Africa, bitterly opposed to the move for a republic and in mourning for what, to them, is a final political break with the Mother Country, but with no clear alternative policy on the racial issue.

If we ask which expectations are likely to be aided – the triumph of apartheid or its defeat – by the South African withdrawal from the Commonwealth, the only thing that can be safely and sadly predicted is that victory in the apartheid struggle, whichever way it goes, is likely to cost more blood now, both white and black, than it would have done if somehow South Africa could have been kept within the counsel and compromise of Commonwealth association.

What of the effect of this withdrawal on the strength of the Commonwealth itself? Here, I think, Dr Verwoerd is quibbling when he speaks about the disintegration of the Commonwealth. Special South African economic bonds, and even some aspects of legal bonds, for instance as to immigration, may be continued on a bilateral basis with Commonwealth countries. More important is the breach of the psychological and traditional bonds of this group of nations. And here it may be that the South African withdrawal, while finally separating her from her sister countries, will strengthen the bonds between the rest of the Commonwealth.

The Commonwealth group in the General Assembly represents one of the few bright hopes of preventing the peoples of the world from reducing themselves to mutually suspicious or even hostile blocs – communist, Western, Arab or Afro-Asian blocs, white or coloured.

Even when the white member countries of the Commonwealth voted differently from its Asian members, the practice of consultation among the Commonwealth delegations in New York provided a potentially important stream of influence, which spanned the blocs.

With last week's admission of Cyprus and Sierra Leone, added to India, Pakistan, Ceylon, Ghana, Malaya, Nigeria, the Commonwealth now has eight coloured members, along with only four white, the United Kingdom, Canada, Australia and New Zealand.

I am myself inclined to think that, with the disruptive influence of white member loyalty to South Africa now removed, the influence on international affairs of the remaining Commonwealth countries will grow in power and depth. And if leaders like Nehru, Nkrumah and Tunku Abdul Rahman grow to realise their full stature as mediators between the new Asian and African nations and the British and American countries, the Commonwealth grouping may well become the stage on which they will play their most decisive role.

For this reason, I rather disagree with Mr Menzies' pessimistic statement at the weekend, that the South African case will cause trouble as a bad precedent for Commonwealth members meddling in each other's domestic affairs. For it can be only a limited precedent, insofar as South Africa herself agreed to the present discussions, and also was seeking readmission as a republic. It could not therefore, as Mr Menzies fears, be a precedent for discussion of the White Australia policy, unless Australia in similar circumstances agreed to it.

Not only are these contingencies unlikely, but I believe that the Asian members have no such implacable hostility to Australia's policy of strict control of immigration from Asia, as they have to apartheid. Some of them have objections to the name rather than the policy; but it is most significant that the Malayan Prime Minister, on the same day as Mr Menzies expressed his fears, said that he supported the White Australia policy, because, he said, if Australia were to open its doors, it would be swamped in no time, and 'that would be unfair to the Australian people'.

Hijackers and Pirates; Spacemen; Revolutionaries

Wednesday 26 July 1961, Notes on the News, 1.15pm 2BL

I suppose that words like 'piracy' and 'hijacking' still set the hearts of some youngsters pounding with the excitement, though most of them I suppose have transferred their allegiance to Sputniks and Explorers, and lately the American Midas III reconnaissance satellite.

I hope, though, that there may still be some simple-minded youngsters who, like myself, thrill at the mention of pirates and hijackers.

Unidentified Cuban 'pirates' are reported to have pressed a gun to the head of the pilot of a scheduled Electra aircraft of the large American Eastern Airlines worth a million and a half pounds, and compelled him to fly the aircraft southward from Miami to Havana, instead of north-west to Dallas, in Texas.

The clear connection between the Cuban government and the so-called piracy, thus far, is that Dr Castro has been coveting some expensive American planes to use in bargaining for the return of several Cuban planes which have been put under court order in the United States for non-payment by the Cuban government of its debts. Castro called this American legal process 'hijacking', and in a recent speech he virtually invited Cubans to steal and bring in American planes.

In boldness of spirit, the seizure of this Electra plane, while in flight over American soil, is certainly piratical. Even when an American jet fighter plane intercepted it, there was not a tremor in the Cuban hand which held the pistol against the temples of Pilot Buchanan, and all that the fighter could do was to waggle its wings at the Electra, which didn't impress the gunman either.

I don't want to destroy youngsters' illusions about 'piracy' in the air. But I must still say that in law, this is probably not a case of piracy at all. The classical pirate is a person who on the high seas, or operating from the high seas, commits acts of violence without the authority of a government, and (probably also) for private rather than public ends.

If the enterprising gentlemen with the gun were agents of the Cuban government, then this was clearly not piracy, but just a particularly flagrant breach of American sovereignty over its territory, not to speak of unlawful seizure of the plane.

Even if the Cuban government did not authorise the seizure, this was still probably not piracy, for two reasons: One is that the gunmen were almost certainly acting in the public interests of Cuba rather than to line their own pockets. The other is that the hold-up was not on the high seas or in any other place analogous to the high seas, but in American territorial air space.

As between the Cuban and United States governments, it probably makes little difference whether we regard the gunmen as pirates or not. In either case, there is a serious breach of international law, and the United States is entitled to demand the return of the plane and due amends and compensation for any complicity by the Cuban government.

For the gunmen themselves, however, it might make an important difference whether they were pirates. For under international law, any state in the world which captures a pirate is entitled to try him and punish him – even capitally – because he is said to be 'the enemy of the whole human race'.

Since our youngsters probably are now very disillusioned about Cuban pirates, and I haven't the time to talk about 'hijackers', we had better turn to spacemen. Spaceman Gagarin, after his triumphant visit to London, when he was received by the Queen, is now enjoying another hero's welcome in Havana. He got wet through yesterday saluting in the rain and it is to be hoped that he didn't catch cold, because the Castro Government have arranged for him to lead a million Cubans in celebrating the eighth anniversary of the beginning of Castro's revolutionary struggle against Dictator Batista.

I was much struck on my recent visit to the United States by how many of the Cuban refugees are people who began as friends and even enthusiasts for Castro's revolution. Does the flight of so many supporters indicate that the revolutionary government has lost popular support? And would this mean that Castro's regime is weakening?

This is a big question, but two preliminary things are worth saying. One is the fact that baiting the big United States can become as unifying a national activity as bullfighting, especially if you think there is a Big Brother standing by to help you if the bull gets out of hand. The other is that while Cubans, like many South Americans, are always glad to overthrow by force a government they get tired of, they also always try to make sure that the leader of the rebels will win before they get onto his side. Castro was a popular hero, leading a bedraggled band in the mountains for years, before he could stir any real Cuban popular movement to help him against Batista. The people really marshalled to him only when Batista's army deserted him.

The publicly announced decision of the Arab League countries to raise volunteers to help Tunisia expel the French from the Bizerte base has, for an international lawyer, the same kind of comic opera flavour as the talk of pirates and hijacking between Cuba and the United States.

In the old-fashioned days which we now denounce as nasty power politics, a state was either in a war or out of it. If it was not in it, then it mustn't send troops to fight in the war, though it would not be held responsible if its individual citizens went abroad as individuals, to volunteer for service with a belligerent.

In our own topsy-turvy world, where states are supposed to have renounced war and violence against each other, Tunisia has attacked the French base at Bizerte, which France holds under binding agreement with Tunisia, and has then complained to the United Nations because naughty France defends herself by defending the base.

And the Arab states who use war and force whenever they can get away with it, but declare that force is illegal whenever they start something they can't finish, have now formally announced that they will raise and send volunteers to help Tunisia against France. But if the Arab states are sending their men to fight, then they are not volunteers. Sending them would amount to an intervention by the Arab states, which France would be entitled (if she wished) to treat as an act of war. But if France did, I have no doubts that Egypt would appeal to the Security Council against naughty, naughty France, which thus violated the Charter of the United Nations.

West Berlin – Shop Window of Democracy

Friday 25 August 1961, Notes on the News, 1.15pm 2BL

The three commandants of the western sectors in Berlin are deploying their 11,000 troops within sight of the wall of staggered roadblocks, barbed wire and bricked up windows and doors, by which East German authorities are seeking to hem in their own population.[1]

Obviously 11,000 troops, even if well-equipped and supported by Centurion and Patton tanks and armoured troop carriers and cars, is a negligible force when ranged against the many divisions which Russia and East Germany could, without difficulty, send across from East to West Berlin. Just as obviously, the improvised boundary wall thrown across the city would not prevent major military movement from East Berlin to West, or, for that matter, vice versa. And Berlin as a whole is surrounded by East German territory.

Up to yesterday, the East German authorities appear to have been scrupulously careful not to interfere with western rights of access to East Berlin, or across the wide corridor from West Germany to West Berlin. They blocked only the access of their own citizens from East to West Berlin.

Strictly speaking, the measures were defensive steps in political rather than military warfare. For beyond question, the flood of East Germans seeking refuge in the western part of the city threatened the communist powers with a political humiliation and defeat of the first magnitude.

By saying that these measures were defensive, I do not mean that they responded to any recent offensive operations by the Western powers. They are a response rather to the long-term economic and ideological offensive against East Germany communism, for which the special four-power status of Berlin is a main strategic base.

For Willy Brandt, the dynamic mayor of West Berlin, Chancellor Adenauer himself and successive administrations in Washington have correctly seen free access between East and West Berlin as a most effective bridgehead for the peaceful penetration of European communist states by democratic ideas.

This is what Mayor Brandt meant when, during a previous crisis, he likened West Berlin to a shop window of democratic success. In this window, hundreds of thousands of East Berliners daily see and take back news of West German achievement, news that

---

1   Construction of the Berlin Wall started on 13 August 1961.

spreads through East Germany, Poland, other satellite countries, to Russia itself. At moments, as in 1956 and now again in 1961, this can lead to unrest in citizens of the communist states. How seriously Moscow takes this unrest should still be fresh in our memories from the East German and Hungarian affairs of 1955–56.

The present phase of the Berlin affair centres on the communist attempt to board up the democratic display window that is West Berlin. This is the real point behind the Western protest against the ban on movement of East Germans. By any standards, of course, to ban tens of thousands of East Germans from going where they want to go is a violation of human rights. But, after all, this kind of thing has been chronic in communist countries for years without too much Western protest, and some Western countries have also, for that matter, felt it necessary to impound the passports or otherwise check the movement of their own citizens.

The present East German ban is aimed, of course, not at preventing political activity of individuals abroad, but to stop the flood of refugees from East Germany from creating a major internal crisis there. The flight of people, like the flight of money, is infectious: the flight of money leads to economic collapse, the flight of people leads to both economic and political collapse.

Had the flood continued to swell, even violent rebellion in East Germany could not have been ruled out. While this would have clinched political victory for Washington and Bonn, I doubt whether Washington would have welcomed it, for the political victory might have been very dangerous militarily. Washington does not want to be faced again, as it was in Hungary, with the bitter choice between, on the one hand, starting a general war by helping armed rebellion in a Soviet satellite and, on the other hand, having to stand by shamefaced, while Soviet forces ruthlessly crushed the rebels.

These are the deeper issues underlying Western debate about counter-measures to the East German ban on movement of its citizens. Until yesterday, as I have said, freedom of Western access to East Berlin had not been infringed, or even threatened, except by the East Germans designating particular places of entry to Berlin for different classes of civilian, diplomatic and military traffic.

This morning's news that Russia has now complained that the Western powers are abusing their rights of access to West Berlin from West Germany may therefore herald a new and more dangerous phase of the crisis. The Soviet charge is that subversive agents and propagandists are being flown in by West Germany and the other Western powers. But its real meaning is either that Moscow remains worried about the unrest in East Berlin and needs a whipping-boy in case things get out of hand there; or that it is preparing the way for a cold-blooded blockade of West Berlin similar to that of the late 1940s.

On the whole, I think the former, less alarmist view, is the correct one, which gives us a moment to consider whether the fact that the boundary between East and West Berlin is sealed to East Berliners decreases the danger of local or general war over Germany? And whether it improves or worsens the Western negotiating position?

I would say that the East German ban does not increase the danger of war, though obviously it does not remove it. I would also say that the ban rather improves the Western negotiating position than otherwise, and this for four reasons.

First, the issue of access across the corridor from West Germany to the four million people of Berlin is not yet involved. Second, the immobilisation of East Berliners, though a tragedy and a breach of human rights, reduces the danger that the East German authorities will be driven to provoke a showdown with the West, as a diversion from political collapse at home. Third, the sealing of the boundary and the deployment of Western forces along it, though it does not prevent deliberate large-scale military movements, does provide a kind of trip-wire which will reduce the risk of accidental military clashes. Finally, even though the West Berlin window is boarded up, the advantage in political warfare remains with the West, for East Germans still remember what is behind the boards, and may hanker after it even more. And this unrest among East Germans also has military importance, for it is likely to deter Moscow from its most likely military plan, namely that of using East German guerrillas as a cat's paw for laying hold of West Berlin.

Kennedy Proposes Disarmament

Wednesday 27 September 1961, Notes on the News, 1.15pm 2BL

President Kennedy's speech to the General Assembly bears on the immediate international crisis at three main points.

The first is its proposal for an immediate nuclear tests ban as part of a new plan for total disarmament by stages. This plan throws the surprise attack and nuclear test questions back into the general disarmament pot, as part of a first phase which would also include reduction of rocket manufacture and of conventional armies, and creation of a body to police disarmament.

To understand the meaning of all this you have to recall the weary history since 1946, when the Security Council established the first nuclear disarmament committee. It failed. Then the General Assembly urged direct Great Power negotiations, in which over the years it was found necessary to take nuclear and conventional disarmament together. After hundreds of meetings, some broad disarmament principles were agreed, but deadlock remained on how to implement them.

Finally, Moscow and Washington tested the hope that they might break the deadlock by concentrating on two smaller questions. These were the prevention of surprise attacks, and the banning of nuclear weapon tests. The hope was that successes here would relieve tension and slow down the arms race. These negotiations too were protracted and finally petered out – first the surprise attack, and then the test ban talks only last month.

At the end of August, when Soviet delegate Tsarapkin finally scuttled the test ban talks, the Western states had just made important concessions about small nuclear tests, and about the constitution and voting of the test ban control commissions, even agreeing to the Soviet demand for a kind of troika there.

But Tsarapkin blew the talks sky-high by charging that the West was simply out to create 'a ... network of intelligence and spying on the Soviet Union in the guise of a control system', and refused to discuss the test ban further, except as part of general talks for complete disarmament.

One way to understand the President's disarmament plan, therefore, is to see it as an acceptance, willy-nilly of this Soviet throwback, of all questions into the general disarmament chaos. And Wednesday's slogan of 'a peace race to the goal of general and complete disarmament' also has a Khrushchev-like ring.

Does this mean that we can expect dramatic progress towards agreement? I doubt this. For even the first phase of the President's plan requires an effective policing body to be set up; and policing is a chronic cause of breakdown throughout. Moscow Radio has just denounced the whole plan. And, almost as I talk, Soviet delegate Gromyko has declared that it is not a real disarmament plan, and objected precisely to that control element.

Still, it is a big concession that the new plan does not stipulate too much perfection before moving out of the first and into the second phase, in which there would be further reduction of conventional armies, and nuclear stockpiles, and military bases. And the plan also aims at limiting the nuclear club and offers, in effect, not to supply nuclear arms to West Germany. These factors, and also the pressure of neutrals in the General Assembly still, I think, keep the door open for further negotiations.

On East Germany it is difficult to assess how much the President has softened the Western position. East Germany's sealing off East Berlin is already a fait accompli. The ticklish questions are not whether the Soviet Union can suppress unrest in East Germany, but what are to be the guarantees of the West's access routes to West Berlin if it does, and whether the West's recognition of East Germany will strengthen West German trends to try to negotiate with Moscow for reunification of Germany. Would West Germany's link with NATO and the West survive the fadeout of Chancellor Adenauer from the political scene? Significantly, the most conciliatory part of Mr Gromyko's speech this morning was about West Berlin, where he agreed that a limited United Nations force might have status.

On the third of the issues addressed by the President, the UN Secretary-Generalship, the President's speech squarely opposed the Soviet demand for a three-man Secretary-General – one Western, one Soviet and one neutralist. And the final Soviet attitude on the Secretary-Generalship will be a good test of whether Russia really wants to put the United Nations to work.

We should realise that the Soviet troika plan is not a joke, but a deadly serious Russian reaction to UN developments since the Korean affair, which in 1950 made clear that the Security Council, as the peace enforcing body, would be paralysed were Washington and Moscow to be at loggerheads. The General Assembly has been trying ever since to do the job thus left in default. But the Assembly, unlike the Security Council, has no centralised binding power over members, and depends on voluntary contributions from them, for instance, of military contingents. When crisis strikes, most of the 99 members of the UN are stirred in the heat of crisis to confer vital powers on the Secretary-General. Then, when the heat subsides, they can agree neither to tell him what to do, nor to revoke his powers. This gives the office an enormous de facto power in critical situations, but it also offers the chance (though far from any certainty) that the UN could be made to work despite the paralysis of the Security Council.

The Soviet troika plan, in which three joint Secretaries-General would check and balance each other, would also tend, of course, to paralyse that office. And that is why, I think, you can judge any state's intentions about the United Nations by asking whether it wants a Secretary-General or insists to the bitter end on a troika.

The Challenge of Nuclear Testing; Nobel Peace Laureate 1961

Thursday 26 October 1961, Notes on the News

According to calculations of the American Nobel Prize Winner for Chemistry from the University of California, the recent Soviet nuclear tests will cause just under half a million deaths in the next few generations, from genetic causes before or shortly after birth, or from cancer and leukaemia in older persons.

Interpreting these calculations yesterday, Dr Fraser of the CSIRO said that while the short-range effects would last from ten to 40 years, the long-range increase in radioactivity could go on for from 5,000 to 6,000 years. The long-range effects include the gradual re-entry of elements from hundreds of miles up in the atmosphere on to places of human habitation, and working through into human food and drink of distant and remote elements of the globe and its surroundings.

Less than half a million lives scattered over 40 years does not seem so terrible, compared to the estimated 60–100 million Americans or Russians who could be destroyed within a few hours by a surprise nuclear attack of one country on the other. But it is terrible enough, especially if you remember the fact that additions of radioactivity to our environment are cumulative over long periods, and its effects are rather irreversible, and likely to remain so, as far as we can at present see.

By any standards, the Soviet action is all the more deplorable because of the cold-blooded manner in which it was undertaken. The Soviet deliberately broke off the test ban talks and began the series of tests culminating this last 'big bang', a 30 megaton explosion with a dispatch which made clear that elaborate preparations for the tests had been completed even while the talks were going on.

They persisted in test after test, despite protests and pleas not only from the West, but from the neutralist powers gathered in Belgrade. And to crown it all, it would appear that the Soviet Union chose United Nations Day as the day to demonstrate that nothing was going to deter her. While the delegates at the General Assembly were preparing for or celebrating United Nations Day, she exploded her 30-million-tons-of-TNT nuclear bomb not on the ground, much less under the ground, where the spread of radioactivity is kept at a minimum, but well up in the atmosphere, where the spread is worst, and whence much of it will be carried by the winds to other parts of the earth, and even greater quantities will continue to be precipitated over the earth in the good rain for which we used to thank heaven.

It is ironic that, in perpetrating this offence, the Soviet Union has brought home once again the lesson which in the old days used to be proclaimed by prophets and other religious teachers, and in more recent days has been spoken to the world over and over again by scientists like Linus Pauling. Few of us really took in the lessons either of the prophets or the scientists. The lesson now emphasised in deeds is that mankind has acquired powers which make the doings of men in any part of the globe important to everyone else, everywhere else. And even if men project their irresponsibility or their evil designs into the stratosphere the consequences come back to us in the rain for which we used to pray.

Quite apart, therefore, from the more sensational perils of sudden or lingering destruction, and from the deplorable possibility that this 'big bang' was not made in search of scientific information, but in hard bargaining about West Berlin, there is reason to stop and think a while here.

I mean that we must come to think more, and more continually, about the vastly increased moral responsibility which our generation bears. The moral responsibilities of men alive at any moment have undergone a vast expansion in space and time, corresponding to the expanding range of man's dominion. The expansion in space is symbolised by the vehement vigilance all over the globe for signs of the Nova Zembla explosions in each people's homeland; and the expansion in time by the 5,000–6,000 years, during which scientists estimate that the consequences will continue to work themselves out.

But there are as yet no signs among the leaders of the nations that they will quickly meet the challenge of the teaching of the 'Big Bangs', any more than they did that of the prophets and the scientists. Indeed, for me the most horrifying aspect of this whole affair is the role played by the Asian and African delegations, especially the so-called uncommitted ones, during the few days of notice which Moscow gave of its intention to explode these super bombs.

Eight states, including the Scandinavian states and Iceland, Canada, Japan, Pakistan and Iraq, sponsored a resolution expressing deep concern at the Soviet intention and appealed to Moscow not to carry it out. And in view of the urgency of the matter, they sought priority for debate of the resolution.

In the General Assembly, the Asian and African states along with communist bloc have nearly 50 votes. Very little therefore can be done in which the Asians and African votes are not crucial.

The first shock in recent days was that despite the high-sounding talk that is always coming from these states about their being uncommitted because they are concerned with the whole world, and not with either military bloc, the neutralist states made no move to protest or appeal to Khrushchev themselves. Krishna Menon of India made only the milk and water statement that India's opposition to all nuclear testing was unchanged.

But even worse was yet to come when these states sullenly (and I hope shamefacedly) refused to say that the eight-nation resolution was an urgent one, entitled to priority. And, even as they rebuffed it, United Nations Day dawned, and the 30 megaton bomb went off.

Only after it went off, this morning cables tell us, have these nations finally faced their responsibility and given priority to the resolution, even then with 22 abstentions.

I hope that my own interpretation of this is not correct, that the so-called neutralist nations will always kowtow to the side in the nuclear war whose leadership is the most irresponsible; the one who makes the worst threats and shows himself capable of carrying them out. For even allowing that many of them, as neighbours of Russia, have to be careful, such an attitude would be a great disaster for themselves, for the United Nations and for all mankind.

This is the reality, I believe, that lay behind the Soviet troika proposal for a three headed Secretary-General – one Western, one communist and one neutralist. For I feel sure that Mr Khrushchev's estimate was that the Soviet head could make a fiercer and more frightening face than could the Western, so that in any crisis which really mattered, the neutralist head, and therefore the United Nations, would come out on the Soviet side.

Moscow half yielded this point when it agreed with Washington on the appointment as interim Secretary-General of the Burmese, U Thant. But it is still negotiating toughly about the number and nationalities of the Assistant Secretaries-General who are to act as the new Secretary-General's day-to-day adviser.

Finally a word about Zulu Chief Luthuli who has just belatedly been awarded the Nobel Peace Prize for 1960. I think you might be interested to know that some people in Australia, of whom I was one, pressed his name on the Nobel Peace Committee.

In my letter of 1 July 1960 to the committee I wrote this:

The lifetime of steady dedication of Luthuli to the settlement, on a basis of peace and mutual accommodation, of perhaps the most intractable racial conflict of our time, is a matter of public record. In the leadership by Chief Luthuli of his own people, in their struggle for a just social order in South Africa, he has shown the greatest loyalty and courage in stating and pressing their case. Yet he has presented their case, not in a partisan spirit regardless of the just claims of other sections of the population, but as one concerned above all to guide all his fellow men, whatever their racial origins, into the paths of non-violence and mutual respect and helpfulness. Insofar as their different situations permit, it is correct to regard Luthuli as playing somewhat of the role which the Mahatma Gandhi played in the guidance of Indian nationalism; and the potential world role of the African continent, therefore, also bespeaks his greatness in his generation.

It is such a pity that the award was not made in 1960 when South Africa still had some bridges to cross in its apartheid policy.

The Future of Britain's Base in Singapore

Friday 23 November 1961, Notes on the News

The United Kingdom-Malayan discussions in London, concerning future use of the UK's Singapore base under the Greater Malaysia Federation, have ended well.

After the great shock of Singapore's fall in World War II, many people, including military experts, doubted its strategic value in future conflicts. These doubts have been increased and complicated by recent revolutionary developments in weapons, particularly nuclear craft and nuclear weapons; as well as by the obvious interest in the area of two great neighbouring land powers, the Soviet Union and mainland China. The Soviet Union, as recent rumours of operations in the Pacific and Russia remind us, undoubtedly has a very formidable submarine fleet. While mainland China has not yet become an important naval power, she has great land power and many opportunities of penetration by land from bases controlled by friendly regimes in Southeast Asia. Air transport now allows land power to be extended to points that formerly could only be reached by naval power. These techniques are available to both Moscow and Peking; and Peking has many potential fifth columns in the general area, in the solid masses of people of Chinese origin, for example in Singapore itself.

Despite the pessimists, Singapore Naval Base still remains a base, 16 years after World War II. At various stages indeed in the development of SEATO, the Southeast Asia Treaty Organisation, the question has been warmly debated between the United Kingdom and the United States, whether Singapore or Manila should serve as the main SEATO base. In a sense Manila won the day; but strictly speaking even Manila is not so much a SEATO as a US base, as Singapore is a British base. The fact is that SEATO itself has never become a standing military organisation in the sense that NATO has.

Malaya, in its still-young existence as a separate independent state, initially had no say as to the use of the Singapore base. She has raised the matter now as part of her proposal for a single federation of Malaya and Singapore, Borneo, Sarawak and Brunei. The London talks also worked out an agreed procedure for negotiating the federation, probably in the next two or three years. But the main problem was the future of the base.

The Malayan Prime Minister was pulled different ways by conflicting anxieties. His dominant concern was that the closing of the base would deprive Singapore of much of its wealth, and a great section of its people, of their means of livelihood. As chief partner in the new federation, Malaya wants to keep that source of revenue. But, on the other hand, Malaya (like India) has stayed out of SEATO, and did not wish to become involved indirectly through possible SEATO use of the base. Prime Minister Tunku Abdul Rahman proclaimed this loudly before the conference.

The Malayan bugbear, therefore, was the military link with SEATO, not the link with Britain. Malaya, as a matter of fact, both before and after independence, welcomed and still receives British (and Australian) military help in dealing with internal communist threats.

The friendly compromise that has now been reached is thus no surprise, though it is rather more conciliatory on Tunku Abdul Rahman's part than was expected. Yesterday, the pundits were still prophesying that Malaya would demand the right virtually to veto any movement of troops based in Singapore outside the Malaysian Federation. The terms actually reached limit the use of the base to the protection of Southeast Asia, the Commonwealth and the Malaysian Federation itself. Obviously, that is a very wide and flexible mandate. With quite significant exceptions, indeed, it would permit the British forces based in Singapore to engage in exactly the same operations as if they were SEATO forces. But they must do so as forces of the United Kingdom or of the Commonwealth and not as SEATO forces.

This relatively happy outcome draws attention to the pride, which Britain may properly feel about her relations with her former colonies. Despite a long and bitter independence struggle, I found that friendship for Britain and Britons is as warm in India as anywhere in the world. Malaya's warmth is a close second to India's, as was shown yesterday when the Malayan delegate in the General Assembly opposed a Soviet bid to fix early target dates for the independence of all remaining colonial peoples and territories.

The speech made by Malayan delegate Ahmed Kamil might have come from the United Kingdom delegation itself. Explaining why he thought British assurances adequate, he declared that the Commonwealth grew as the British Empire shrank, and that it was a good example of the cordial transfer of power from a colonial authority to its dependent peoples. It opened up, he said, 'a new vista of happy relations and cooperation between them as equal partners in the world community of sovereign nations.'

The Samos satellite secretly launched yesterday by the United States is mooted to have included a Midas III spy satellite capable of detecting missiles at their launching pads. This would be the third spy satellite designed to overfly the Soviet Union, and you may wonder why there has not been a loud Soviet hue and cry like she made about the U2 spy plane 18 months ago.

The main point is that Soviet sovereignty above its territory, like that of other states, extends only to the limits of the airspace. Spy planes use the airspace and are therefore trespassing when over another state's territory. But a satellite operates outside the airspace; indeed, its speed would burn it up in the air. It flies beyond the legal domain of any state, even though it may do virtually the same job as a spy plane.

Goa, the Indian Conquest

Thursday 21 December 1961, Notes on the News, 1.15pm 2BL

When Adlai Stevenson declared in the Security Council debate that it would bring the death of the United Nations if the flagrant Indian violation of the Charter by its attack on Goa was condoned, he was speaking high politics as well as law.

The Indian delegate in the Security Council declared that the Charter could not prevent India from protecting the 360,000 Hindus in Goa; and the Soviet delegate clapped its 99th veto on a resolution calling for a ceasefire and an Indian withdrawal.

The call for a ceasefire was too late, for the small Portuguese force of 3,000 men had already been overwhelmed by a massive Indian force of 30,000. And, in terms which recalled the most imperialist imperialisms in India, the subjugation of Goa and the neighbouring territories of Daman (of which the tiny enclaves of Dadra and Nagar-Haveli are a part) and Diu, had been announced.

But what about Indian withdrawal? The nearest that the League of Nations ever came to an agreed definition of aggression was to say that the side which refused to withdraw to its frontier was an aggressor. But obviously India will not willingly withdraw, for the very purpose of her military operations was to commit an act of conquest of the territory of another state.

There have been great debates in the United Nations, too, about the meaning of aggression. But there is one thing that is absolutely clear under the Charter. This is that to send your forces across a frontier in order to conquer and annex the territory of another state is a violation of Article 2, paragraph 4, even if you try to call it only 'anti-colonial liberation'. That paragraph squarely forbids the use of force against the territorial integrity of any state.

What is the Indian side of the story? The leaflets dropped over Goa in advance of the invading armies declared that these armies were invading Goa 'to defend the honour, the security of the Motherland' from which Goa had been 'separated too long'. 'Motherland' sounds too much like 'Fatherland' and too little like Mother India. But 'separated too long' is correct enough.

Portugal has been in Goa since 1510, and her rights there were recognised by the International Court of Justice as recently as 1960. Only a 'temporary administration', the Soviet delegate called it – 'temporary' for 450 years. However anti-colonial we are, and however much we might have hoped that Portugal would peacefully hand it over to India, the fact remains that Goa was not legally part of the Republic of India. The mere fact that India became tired of asking Portugal to transfer Goa does not entitle India to take it by force.

The claim, moreover, that these tiny areas, amounting to about 1500 square miles in all, with a population of 600,000 surrounded by a vast ocean of 430 million Indians, threatened India's security, answers itself. The Indian conquest of the tiny garrison took about 30 hours.

Even more fantastic is the claim that India had to invade Goa in order to protect her 'territorial integrity' there. This is rather like a highwayman's plea that he did the hold-up to protect his property rights in the victim's purse.

Through his campaign for the principles of non-violence and negotiation for mutual benefit, the great Gandhi endeared India and himself to all mankind. Nehru and the Republic of India have ceaselessly rammed these principles down the throats of Western states. Only five years ago, Nehru and his Afro-Asian colleagues flayed Britain alive for trying to defend, with arms, her Suez life-line. But with all its rashness and ineptitude, Britain at least had reason to think that Egypt was violating her legal rights, and that her vital economic interests were in danger. She did not go in to take a slice of Egypt, nor did her conduct mock the Charter.

This contrast of Suez and Goa is a main symptom of the mortal sickness, which Stevenson sees as threatening the United Nations. If the United Nations were not to condone the Indian adventure in Goa, when it acted so vigorously in the more excusable case of Suez, only one inference would be possible. The UN would be acting as a straitjacket to stop Western states protecting their lawful interests, while holding the ring for non-Western states to use force to pursue theirs. And one suspicious sign that this may become the case, is that while Moscow rattled its atom bombs to restrain Britain, it now rattles its bombs and flourishes its vetoes to encourage and protect India's lamentable resort to force.

Unless the General Assembly gives the lie to this kind of double standard and double talk, the future of the United Nations will be just as grim as Adlai Stevenson thinks. No society can last in which some members who use force are treated as crusading heroes, and others with cause no less good, as criminals. 'Put and take' used to be a good game; but 'You put – we take' isn't a game at all. It's just a swindle.

Moral Challenges from the Congo and West New Guinea

Friday 19 January 1962, Notes on the News

Scenes of oppression and war are now being enacted on the world stage, not by the biggest powers but by other, lesser powers. Who are these players whose manoeuvrings now threaten war, violate the Charter and flout the principles of peaceful settlement? And which nations are now acting blithely as if might is right, and as if self-determination of peoples doesn't matter? And what has become of self-determination as a principle of the United Nations anyhow?

The hideous massacre of priests in the Congo, the latest instance this oppression, was apparently committed by soldiers of the Nationalist Congolese Army, which arrived in Katanga a week after Christmas, as a part of combined campaign of the UN Command and the Central Congolese government, to force Katanga fully into the Congo Federation. The priests were Belgian missionaries, but not even the most extreme Congolese centraliser could mistake them for the Belgian mercenaries who are still supposed to be the colonial thorn in the side of Congolese unity.

Whether these soldiers acted under orders or were on a frolic of their own, their acts remind us of the fantastic situation into which the anti-colonialist campaign of the Afro-Asian and Soviet blocs has manoeuvred the United Nations, and the world itself. With their mass of small state votes in the General Assembly, and the skilful exploitation of Moscow-US tensions, they have steadily pushed the UN and the world itself into impossible positions.

One is the overt policy that all colonial peoples must be given independence immediately regardless of their readiness or capacity to govern themselves, even if they are neither in a position to maintain internal law and order, nor able to defend themselves externally, and even if (as in the Congo) tribal wars are still the daily order of things.

And since both Moscow and Washington are each determined to keep the other out of such a power vacuum, the still-weak United Nations Secretary-General is left to struggle as best he can with problems which include, in the Congo, the very establishment of some kind of stable state.

> What was wicked for a Western colonial power has become a sacred duty for an African colonial power … The Indonesian drive for West New Guinea, the Indian drive for Goa … Communist China's pressure on India's frontiers, all present the same tragic pantomime. Asian powers who have been preaching for years the awful wickedness of force and domination by the western nations take naturally and self-righteously to the same kind of thing.

On what principle is he to act in such a situation? We might imagine that, whatever else was disputed, the principle of self-determination would be unquestioned basis for United Nations action. But whose self-determination? The Katangans under President Tshombe say they want to be a separate state. Their land is large enough to support a state, and it contains most of the wealth resources of the old Belgian colony. They say they are a separate people, and they don't see why their wealth should go to bolster a vast centralised poverty-stricken Congolese Federation.

The UN Secretary-General, supported by most Asian and African members of the UN, has taken the stand (with the Central Congolese government) that Katanga must at all costs duly enter the Federation. How this marches with the principle of self-determination, I have never understood. Nor can I think of any way in which the Katangans could demonstrate, more clearly than they have, that what they want to do is to control their own lives and society. They have taken support from wherever they could get it, including Belgian mercenaries – so would we in their position!

In fact, the only principle that makes sense of the contrary position of the UN and the Central government is that the Central Congolese government is entitled to replace the Belgian colonial power. While ending the old colonial imposition, the new Congo state seems to be imposing itself on unwilling peoples. What was wicked for a Western colonial power has become a sacred duty for an African colonial power.

The Indonesian drive for West New Guinea, the Indian drive for Goa (now completed by violence), Communist China's pressure on India's frontiers, all present the same tragic pantomime. Asian powers who have been preaching for years the awful wickedness of force and domination by the western nations take naturally and self-righteously to the same kind of thing at the first opportunity.

The UN Secretary-General, U Thant, yesterday for the first time formally offered to mediate between the Netherlands and Indonesia. The final basis for the Indonesian claim to West New Guinea is really that Indonesia is entitled to take over all Dutch colonial power in the area. This is merely a claim to become the next colonial power, for neither ethnically nor in ability to help the Papuans, is Indonesia specially fitted for governing them; and thousands of Papuans are demonstrating against the transfer. U Thant has a tough job ahead of him as mediator.

And when you add today's news that the Indonesian Deputy Naval Chief of Staff was on board one of the torpedo boats sunk by the Dutch, they say in territorial waters, moving in to make a landing, all this is high but grim comedy. This new state, the promoter of the Bandung Principles for peace on earth, declares repeatedly that Indonesia is about to invade West New Guinea, flouts the UN Charter and its pledges to Australia, scorns the principle of self-determination and then complains indignantly that its navy's second-in-command was attacked without the slightest provocation while he was on a perfectly innocent voyage near Dutch New Guinea.

Sceptics used to say 'Tell it to the marines'. I gather that the marines are pretty wise to this sort of thing these days, but I have little doubt that President Soekarno could still tell it, with good effect, to the Asian, African and Soviet blocs in the United Nations General Assembly.

Election in India; Paradox of Colonialism in West New Guinea

Monday 19 February 1962, Notes on the News

The Republic of India is near the middle of a ten-day poll for the election of a new union parliament – the Lok Sabha, as well as the parliaments of the constituent states of the Republic. India follows the British model of a government responsible to parliament, so the elections will also decide which party holds office. But as long as Nehru still leads the Congress Party it is a foregone conclusion that it will be returned.

India is a federal state with a written constitution, for which our own constitution and that of the United States were chief models. In some ways the Indian Constitution is even more elaborate than ours. India has far more member states, with a great variety and conflict of religious and linguistic groups, and the constitution contains the longest bill of rights ever, guaranteeing fundamental rights.

In other ways, however, the Indian federal problem is simpler than ours. The central government's powers are much broader than Canberra's and, even more important, it is quite easy for the central government to amend the constitution, whenever the constitution gets seriously in its way.

But, of course, the most startling facts about the Indian elections are the size and nature of the electorate. Under Nehru's inspiration India accepted manhood suffrage from the start, and manhood suffrage in a country of 430 million people means manhood with a vengeance. Indian villagers love children and believe in having plenty. But even when you have allowed for this, the current incredible figures still give 210 million voters at the present elections.

According to the same figures, 160 million of these voters cannot read or write. Despite this, at each of India's two previous elections in 1952 and 1957, about 50 percent of the electors voted. The illiteracy problem is met by each of the 14 competing parties using a different picture symbol (like a house, or tree or banana or camel) for its campaigning, and the ballot papers listing the same symbols, against the chosen of which the voter rubber stamps his cross.

Besides illiteracy, India's Election Commission has to struggle with the vast scattering of the 160 million peasant voters in remote and inaccessible villages throughout the subcontinent. When I stayed recently with a missionary friend in upper Bombay state, he told me that he found it impossible to get around his parish of 50 villages in less than a year. His converts didn't always last from one visit to the next.

The electoral officers have to service, one way or another, no less than 225,000 polling-booths within ten days. They would of course need powerful telescopic eyes all around their heads to prevent corruptions and abuses, and new procedures are being tried this year to reduce these to a minimum.

All in all, the survival and comparative stability of political democracy in India is a great triumph, of which Nehru and his people are entitled to be very proud, and which is vitally important for the Western world.

But the great test for this democracy is still in the future. The source of danger lies very deep. Democracy may perhaps manage with an illiterate electorate, but it cannot continue very long with electors who have virtually no political awareness, not even sufficient to make demands on politicians. Tens of millions of Indian villagers still have the same kind of indifference to 'the government' as they had to the British Raj, or to the Muslim conquering emperors of centuries ago. They live on the principle that the less they know about the government, and the government about them, the better. Of course, some of us in Australia, say this too, but very few of us really believe it.

All this is perhaps the deepest cause of the anxious question of many friends of India, 'After Nehru, what?' And of their fear that 'After Nehru, the flood'.

External Affairs Minister Paul Hasluck now reports that the peoples of Australian Papua-New Guinea want to continue their association with Australia, and become in due course the seventh Australian state. Fifty years ago, just before World War I, and perhaps even 40 years ago, after World War I, this fact could have been regarded as an assurance of the stable future of the New Guinea peoples. And the same could have been said of the rejection by the People's Council of Dutch West New Guinea of the Indonesian claim that they must accept Indonesian nationality, and their insistence on the right of choosing their own destiny, at latest by 1970.

It is a bitter paradox, however, that the Asian and African states, making up half the present states of the world, after having achieved independence themselves, are now making it very difficult for the remaining dependent peoples to choose their future really freely. However genuine, deep and sincere may be the wishes of the West New Guinea peoples, this will not prevent Indonesia form trying to impose its rule on them, nor prevent Asian and African states, and the Soviet bloc from giving blanket support to Indonesian claims.

And the fact that Papua-New Guinea peoples want to become in due course the seventh Australian state, is rather the beginning than the end of our long-term problems in New Guinea.

Australian Foreign Policy Towards Thailand, West New Guinea

Friday 16 March 1962, Notes on the News

The Australian Parliament, the press and Australians generally are still trying to get the exact meaning of two government statements on critical items of foreign policy – one on Thailand, made on Wednesday night, the other on West New Guinea, made last night. In both of them Sir Garfield Barwick rather spread himself, in the latter to the tune of 28 pages.

The Thailand issue arises from the joint communiqué issued in Washington ten days ago by the Secretary of State and the Thai Foreign Minister. In it, the United States affirmed that it did not regard its obligation to defend Thailand against armed attack as dependent on the prior agreement of other SEATO parties, namely Australia, France, New Zealand, Pakistan, Philippines and the UK.

Australian External Affairs Minister Barwick reacted to this at the time by 'welcoming' it. And this 'Hear, hear!' (as it were) was echoed in Bangkok by Australian Ambassador Booker, as well as by Thai Prime Minister Sarit, who told the press that the US had told Thailand that Australia too might give individual aid.

Since Australia was said to have been consulted before the joint communiqué, parliament and the press began probing as to how far Australia had undertaken an individual military commitment to Thailand. In his written reply in the House of Representatives Sir Garfield seems to say that Canberra's 'Hear, hear' to Dean Rusk did not imply that it had decided on any individual military commitment. It meant only that Canberra agreed with Dean Rusk that each SEATO member would decide for itself when and how it would fulfil its obligations.

If this was all that Dean Rusk meant by his statement, you may well ask why he made it. It would mean not only that Australia alone would decide what its individual military commitment under SEATO to Thailand amounted to if Thailand were attacked, but also that the US would do the same about military help to Australia, if Australia were attacked. Sir Garfield drew his interpretation from the key Article IV (1) of the SEATO Treaty, which says that in the case of aggressively armed attack against a SEATO member each other 'will act to meet the common danger in accordance with its constitutional processes'.

Actually, however, I believe that Canberra's apparent focus on each SEATO member's freedom to decide about acting in defence of another member, under the strict letter of the

Treaty is a distortion of the joint communiqué. For the realities of SEATO are that, apart from certain limited planning and training arrangements (in which by the way the United States and Thailand are the members mainly involved), SEATO has no standing military establishment or headquarters. And I remember saying to you about a year ago (15 January 1961) that 'the modesty of Washington's conceptions of SEATO as a military instrument reflects the high importance which it attaches to having its own hands free to use its own military power' in the area.

In short, Washington already had her great military base at Manila and her fleet disposed along her chain of island defences in the western Pacific. To put military teeth into SEATO, by putting forces at SEATO's collective disposal would, therefore from Washington's viewpoint, merely give to other SEATO members a veto on its use of its own forces in a particular crisis.

Quite apart, therefore, from what the treaties may say, the military reliance that Thailand could place on collective SEATO military action was rather negligible.

Measured by these realities, Dean Rusk's statement, that the United States would defend Thailand against direct communist aggression even if no other SEATO member takes such action, obviously indicates a firming up rather than a weakening of the US military commitment to Thailand. It coincided with a United States delivery of 20 F86 Sabre jet fighters and a number of training planes, with the appointment of General Conway, commander of the 'crack' 82nd Airborne Division, to command the US Military Assistance Group, which is training the Thais in guerrilla warfare, and the easing of Thai pressure for strengthening SEATO by eliminating the unanimity rule. And it also follows the penetration of communist Pathet Lao forces last month to Nam Tha, only 50 miles from the Siamese border.

In this light, Canberra should surely have expected that its loud 'Hear, hear' to the joint communiqué would have been understood to mean exactly what Sir Garfield now says it doesn't mean.

The value to a foreign policy of high-flown phrases which, when clarified, turn out to be verbal facades for chronic indecisions, is dubious. We have had past examples of this on the West New Guinea question, and there was still another in last night's 28-page statement on West New Guinea, though it was in most other respects well balanced.

It declares that no one could mistake what was the Australian view about the use of force by either side in the dispute. But it also says that in such a 'complicated and delicate' situation, when negotiations are proceeding, no responsible government would give any firm commitment about what measures Australia would take in case of hostilities.

There was, it is true, clarity on the related point, that Australia would defend to the utmost her own territories of Papua and New Guinea. This, however, rather made matters worse. For however we cover it with fine words, Djakarta will infer from our threat to use defensive force limited to East New Guinea, a tacit undertaking that we will do nothing but talk if she uses force in West New Guinea. And this at any rate is not a sensible undertaking for us to inject into the 'complicated and delicate situation' to which the minister is so sensitive.

Indonesian Assault on West New Guinea – Critique of Australia's Position

Tuesday 26 March 1962, News Commentary, 6.55pm 2BL

Both the Dutch and Australian Cabinets have been in grave session today, on the West New Guinea dispute. Eleven months ago exactly, Mr Menzies told the House of Representatives that, while he had informed visiting Indonesian General Nasution that Australia had no military arrangements with the Netherlands about West New Guinea, 'armed conflict in that country … would present Australia, in common with other countries, with a grave problem'. And he said this last in substance three times before he sat down.

Mr Menzies put beyond doubt at that time, as far as words could,

1) that Australia recognised Dutch sovereignty in West New Guinea;

2) that Australia insisted on the right to self-determination for all the peoples of New Guinea; and

3) that Australia would not oppose the transfer of Dutch sovereignty to Indonesia by negotiation free of threat and coercion.

And the Prime Minister reported that General Nasution gave him assurances, which renewed those repeatedly made by Indonesian leaders, 'that force would not be used'.

Less than 12 months later, the Indonesian government has openly declared its intentions to use force in West New Guinea, has assigned an army for that purpose, and has already launched two moderately sized invasion ventures. Pressed by her failure to steamroll the General Assembly, and by the Dutch offer to hand the territory to the United Nations, Indonesia recently agreed to enter into secret talks with the Netherlands under US and UN auspices.

Indonesia continued her military activities, however, even while she was supposed to be negotiating. And yesterday she withdrew her representative from the talks. Simultaneously, her spokesmen declared that when Indonesia took over West New Guinea this would provide Australia with a buffer against communism, and that we need never fear that Indonesia will become a communist base. This assurance was given rather ominously by the major general commanding the so-called 'army of liberation' for West New Guinea. This army, if Indonesia's plans succeed, will in due course operate on the international frontier of Australia Papua and New Guinea.

So where are we? What General Nasution sought and got 11 months ago, in return for his promise not to use force, was an assurance that Australia had no advance military commitment to The Hague to help defend West New Guinea. Now, less than a year later, after Djakarta's repudiation in words and action of its pledge not to use force, the Australian government rewards Djakarta with even more generous assurances. In effect, we now say that we will not give the Dutch military aid, whatever force Indonesia cares to use against Dutch New Guinea, provided that the Indonesian liberation army respects the frontiers of Australian sovereignty, and does not try to 'liberate' Australian Papua and New Guinea. This latter, said Sir Garfield 12 days ago, we would defend.

Of course, Australia also recognises Dutch sovereignty in West New Guinea. But Australia, Sir Garfield clearly indicated, would not help to defend that, because the Asian states are on Indonesia's side, and Washington and London are sitting on the fence.

So Canberra rewards Djakarta for resorting to force, by tacitly assuring Djakarta that we will accept whatever it can impose on West New Guinea even by force. And Djakarta's contemptuous rejection of the claims of the West New Guinea peoples to self-determination, is rewarded by Canberra rather 'piping down' on its support of that principle.

What this adds up to in terms of morality and wisdom is a separate and complex question. But, even in terms of Machiavellian expediency, the Australian position is surely rather strange. After all, will Australian sovereignty in East New Guinea be any less objectionably 'colonial' to Djakarta, than is Dutch sovereignty in West New Guinea? Will Asian states be on our side of the quarrel if, in a year or two, Djakarta demands that Australia quit Papua and New Guinea, claiming that our sovereignty there is the last stronghold of colonialism in this region? And does Canberra think that, after a successful Indonesian conquest of West New Guinea, Washington and London are more likely to help us to defend Australian Papua and New Guinea?

Whistling in the dark can be a great comfort. But as the light dawns we should stop whistling, and take a good hard look.

Indonesia Infiltrates West New Guinea – What Should Australia's Policy Be?

Wednesday 11 April 1962, Notes on the News, 1.15pm 2BL

While the Commandant of the West Irian Combat Corps was declaring from Ambon that regular Indonesian troops would soon be on the West New Guinea mainland, and the Dutch authorities there were claiming that small detachments of invading Indonesians had already been captured on Waigeo Island and on the mainland, Djakarta itself had been putting out a very different line. This is that the various naval and land forays against West New Guinea reported over the last few weeks did not involve any Indonesians proper, but rather anti-Dutch Papuans who wished to make common cause with Indonesia.

President Soekarno himself, who only a few weeks ago was making quite unambiguous threats to oust the Dutch by force and declaring the whole nation to be mobilised for war on this account, this week also took a different note, more hopeful for peace. Addressing an air force parade, he now says merely that Indonesia might go to war if the Dutch do not withdraw from West New Guinea by the end of 1962 – that is, he now extends the period of his ultimatum by about eight months.

At the same time, he indicated acceptance in principle of the new US-promoted plan calling for Dutch withdrawal and for a UN control commission in West New Guinea for three years. During this time the Indonesians would replace the Dutch as administrators, but at the end of it there would be a UN guarantee of self-determination for the native peoples thereafter.

This plan and the Indonesian reaction to it, if they are correctly reported and seriously intended, constitute a very considerable step towards a sensible solution, even though the Dutch government is understandably annoyed that the plan was officially submitted to Djakarta before the Dutch government was consulted about it.

What is most puzzling about these late reports is that President Soekarno's virtual postponement of his ultimatum for another eight months was made independently of Dutch reactions to this new plan. Why, after his recent blood and iron stand, should the President now soften both on his ultimatum date and on the self-determination principle? The puzzle is greater in view of the recent Dutch decision to send out substantial reinforcements, some of which are already en route.

Three explanations are possible. The first is that the frequency and near-hysteria of Indonesian threats and demands are a line of political warfare designed to soften up Dutch,

Australian, American and British attitudes. You will remember that Mr Khrushchev has now for years been fixing and then postponing ultimatum dates on the Berlin question. So also Djakarta may think that if the West Guinea issue becomes sufficient of an international nuisance, the diplomatic friends of The Hague can be frightened off, and the Dutch themselves persuaded that the game is not worth the candle.

The second is that Djakarta has sufficient assurance of communist military aid to be confident that she can keep militarily ahead during a prolonged war of nerves. Indeed, one of the Indonesian Government's purposes in the New Guinea affair may be to get support at home and abroad for its own military build-up.

A third explanation is that Djakarta literally meant her immediate military threats earlier this year, but that various reasons now prevent her from carrying them out. One such reason could certainly be the difficulties into which the Indonesian economy has sunk deeper and deeper, since her self-inflicted wounds when she expropriated all Dutch enterprises and broke off all economic and diplomatic relations with The Hague. Only yesterday the Indonesian government announced a danger of famine, and General Nasution has been compelled to cut the preferential pay and rations allocated to the so-called West Irian Liberation Forces.

Indeed, we cannot exclude the possibility that the recent militaristic switch at Djakarta was an attempt to divert domestic grievances of restive, ill-governed Indonesian peoples onto a foreign enemy, and to dull the pangs of hunger with the elation of military adventure and victory, and that this plan has not worked. We must remember in this connection that it is the policy of the Indonesian government not to permit any serious criticism of its policy by the press of Indonesia.

What are we now to make of the opposed arguments in the Australian House of Representatives yesterday, about the UN role in the West New Guinea dispute? The Australian government's position has been that, in view of the stacking of Soviet and Afro-Asian votes against the Netherlands in the General Assembly, it would be useless to bring the matter to the UN, even if force was used by Indonesia. Mr Calwell (said Territories Minister Hasluck) 'ignored the pattern of voting in the United Nations ...'

On the other hand, Deputy Opposition Leader Whitlam charged that Canberra has been slow and inefficient in putting, in the UN, the arguments for the self-determination for West New Guinea. He thought it should be a major Australian objective to bring home to Indonesia through the United Nations its obligations to the peoples of West New Guinea.

I am myself inclined to think that an active and positive policy of renewed initiatives in the UN is still a correct policy for Canberra. And this regardless of whether it makes any difference to the course of the New Guinea dispute. For the big question mark as to the whole future of the UN depends for its answer on whether the organisation can begin to educate its members, and especially the Asian and African members, into moderating their dictatorial bloc attitudes, by respect for Charter principles, and real consideration on the merits of the issues brought before it.

The non-Western blocs have had a good long turn at cooking the Western goose over the fire of Charter principles. But unless they can learn to recognise that what is sauce for the Western goose, is also sauce for the Afro-Asian and communist ganders, what will follow for everybody will not be a feast but a funeral.

Analysis of Indonesia's Claim on West New Guinea

Sunday 23 April 1962, Australia and the World, 12.45pm 2BL

General Nasution has now said openly that Indonesia will go to war if a Papuan state is established in New Guinea. And Senator Dodd of the Foreign Relations Committee sharply criticised what he calls Indonesia's 'arrant baseline claim to New Guinea', and Washington's support of it. These words and Djakarta's weekend hints that President Sukarno will announce next Thursday his refusal to resume Dutch-Indonesian negotiations, invite us to take stock of the legal, moral and political issues.

The independence movement that created Indonesia was accelerated by the Japanese invader in World War II as an act of political warfare. But the political help of the United States and Australia was vital to the Indonesian success in the struggle for independence from 1945 to 1949, during which the Linggadjati, Renville and Round Table Conference Agreements succeeded each other in 1946, 1948 and 1949.

Indonesia finally repudiated the union of the Netherlands and Indonesia under the Dutch Crown envisaged under the Round Table Agreement, cancelled the ancillary economic agreement, virtually confiscated all Dutch property within reach, and broke off all diplomatic relations whatsoever.

The two earlier agreements spoke about the future transfer to Indonesia of what they described as 'the Netherlands Indies', and Indonesia claims that they included West New Guinea. But, well after these early agreements, Indonesia entered into the Round Table Agreement of 1949, which was the only one actually transferring any territory, and this expressly provided that the status quo of West New Guinea should be unchanged, and its future status settled within a year by negotiations.

When it came to these negotiations in December 1950, Indonesia rejected the Dutch proposals, which were in effect for joint Indonesian-Dutch control within the union of the two countries already agreed upon. In later negotiations, Djakarta began to claim that West New Guinea was already legally hers, and that the Dutch were in illegal occupation.

But when Indonesian spokesmen get down to brass tacks, they admit that they have no legal title to West New Guinea, as General Nasution admitted to Mr Menzies only 12 months ago, when he explained that this was why Indonesia has refused Dutch and Australian proposals that the matter be submitted to the International Court.

Still, Indonesia might have a moral right to West New Guinea, even then. For instance, its leaders say that they were led to expect before 1949, that the 'Netherlands Indies' promised to them would include West New Guinea. Their strongest support for this is that in 1946, Lieutenant Governor General van Mook said that New Guinea would not be excluded from the settlement. But the settlement then in view was a Netherlands-Indonesian Union, actually agreed in 1949, and the Dutch offer in 1950 to make West New Guinea a joint territory within the Union, was entirely consistent with this. This offer Indonesia contemptuously rejected, and five years later she repudiated the Union as well.

Again, the Indonesians stake a moral claim based on history. They say that, before Dutch rule, the same native ruler, the Sultan of Tidore, ruled over West New Guinea and some of the adjacent islands of East Indonesia. But in fact, the first political unity within the present boundaries of Indonesia was that imposed by the Dutch colonial power. The Indonesian claim to take whatever the colonial power had taken is really a claim for Indonesia to become a colonial power, in her turn.

This, surely, is an ironic reflection on self-righteous campaigning against colonialism; and it throws cruel and tragic light on the scorn that Djakarta pours on Papuan claims to self-determination, and the present threat to go to war if it is granted.

What of the Indonesian claim on cultural and racial grounds? Obviously the 700,000 Papuans are Melanesian, which Indonesians are not; and the immigrant minority in the west of the country cannot change this. The Indonesian argument amounts to this: Indonesia already contains 17 or so different racial or language groups and, if the West New Guinea peoples are entitled to self-determination, so should the other 17 groups. Mr Menzies said a year ago, after his talks with Nasution, that this amounted to flat rejection of the Papuan right of self-determination. So do I still today; and so do the Papuan people's leaders who are protesting against it.

So far, then, Indonesian claims add up to very little. But it would be unfair to Djakarta not to mention that, in the background, there seems also to be a fear that if the Dutch have a foothold nearby, they may try to reassert their colonial authority over Indonesia proper. Such a fear may have been sincere and understandable during the bitter struggle of the late '40s and early '50s, but scarcely after the Suez Affair, and after the Afro-Asian and communist states came to constitute more than half of the General Assembly.

Much the same point needs to be made as to Indonesia's claim that its objective is the welfare of the peoples of West New Guinea. General Nasution, in his notable interview for the ABC last week, was asked whether Indonesia's difficulties in administering her present territory were not great enough, without the burden of West Papua. He offered little in reply, save a prayer and the claim that Indonesia had raised her own literacy rate dramatically, presumably in the urban areas. What it would do in the very different conditions of New Guinea peoples remains a question.

We must frankly recognise, on the other hand, that the Dutch came later than they should to their present vigorous welfare planning in New Guinea. Yet the change is very great and real. Current Dutch plans are better than Indonesia can hope to implement for decades. The Hague is spending $30 million per annum on the territory and, when she offered last year to transfer the territory to the UN, she also offered to continue to contribute $30 million each year to its advancement.

Even in the middle 1950s, when Indonesia tried and failed to bring General Assembly pressure on The Hague, 41 African, Asian and communist states voted with her.

Twenty-nine members, including most Western and American states, voted against, and 11, including the US, abstained. There were then only 82 members of the UN. Another score of African and Asian states have since been added to the General Assembly, which, in deference to Indonesian intransigence, did not accept last year's generous Dutch offer.

That solution could (in one stroke) have vindicated the self-determination principle, provided funds for West New Guinea development without suspicion of colonialist strings or threats from either side, and above all, settle the dispute without force.

This great UN refusal raises questions even bigger than that of West New Guinea. The General Assembly seems to be virtually conniving at colonial-type adventures by Asian states. Why should Asian states be free to violate principles of self-determination and against the use of force by which Western states are sternly judged?

Double standards will corrupt all UN principles unless they are exposed and banished. No one can be sure whether these trends in the United Nations are reversible. Yet it surely should be a steady and major Australian policy to expose this double standard. And when it comes as near home as New Guinea, Canberra should try to lead Washington and London, rather than slavishly await their indifference.

The West New Guinea dispute, now that it has become a threat to the peace, should be brought to the United Nations on every possible occasion. It is not an answer to say that bloc alignments in the UN prevent this doing any good. It is precisely because such alignments are destroying vital United Nations principles, that the smell of the double standard must be pushed right under members' noses. Asian and African states must learn the same lessons that western states have learned at great sacrifice since 1945.

To allow some members to subvert these principles without exposing the wrong in the General Assembly, is mutual corruption, not mutual education of its members. Australia should stand and be heard on this truth, in the name of both international morality and national policy.

Space Programs of the Great Powers

Friday 5 May 1962, Science Makes News

Together or alone, Washington and Moscow are set on space navigation. The US timetable is for Operation Apollo to make a manned moon landing by 1967–70, but Colonel Glenn's unexpected recent achievement in manually navigating the Mercury craft may even bring the date forward. The Soviet timetable is probably for an earlier date. The choice is whether Washington and Moscow will go on together, or will each go it alone.

The main difficulties about cooperation in space activities resemble those that hamper cooperation in nuclear development. You can't separate all the materials, instruments and know-how for peaceful development from those for warlike purposes. The secrets of guidance systems, heat-resisting structures and instrumentation are common to peaceful and warlike use of powerful rockets and missiles. And, of course, the potential uses of space structures and of observatories on the moon are at least as great for war as for peace. The heat shield for Glenn's Mercury capsule was like that of US ballistic missiles.

An orbiting satellite with modern photography might relay instant intelligence of major structures and movements in states traversed by its frequent orbit. The father of the H-bomb, Edward Teller, has said that an observatory on the moon could know and relay to earth base, all that was going on everywhere on earth. Experts talk of bomb as well as surveillance satellites. Bomb satellites, on instructions from earth, would project themselves at an indicated earth target.

Our session tonight is focused on science, but it would be silly to forget that politics and strategy are bound to affect attitudes in Moscow and Washington to particular kinds of cooperation.

Dr Thornton[1] is certainly right in saying that it would be sensible for Washington and Moscow to join in manned space activities, Washington with its better instrumentation, and Moscow its better booster. But the Russians would probably insist on Russian crew and the question arises whether Washington would expose its secret defence materials and instruments to study by a Russian crew? We must not underrate how many of these problems real co-operation would involve.

---

1   Probably William Edgar Thornton, http://www.jsc.nasa.gov/Bios/htmlbios/thornton-w.html

On the other hand, I agree that the rewards to both countries for overcoming the difficulties would be tremendous. In money alone the cost of putting a man on the moon would be not less than $20,000 million, and could be $100,000 million. Joint work might halve such costs for each; and these countries and mankind as a whole could do much more useful things with this kind of money.

But the money saving would be even greater. If Moscow and Washington keep on competing, then, whichever gets to the moon first, the race will be on for Mars, which might cost as much and more. But if they co-operate, instead of competing, they could together adjust the program for later stages with sensible regard to the priorities on which mankind should spend its resources. I agree that co-operation might speed our arrival on the moon; but it would take the hectic competitive rush out of later space activities.

There would also be other material blessings, like better weather predictions and radio and television relays from orbiting satellites, and possible but still speculative benefits from solar energy, and from mineral or other resources on other planets.

It would also, of course, be a great spiritual blessing if man's entry into space was a peaceful and not a Cold War venture. Co-operation might even spearhead more confidence and friendship on the earthly level.

Of course, we thrill at the prospect of man ceasing to be earthbound, and we admire the intellect, which has opened his way into the vast solar system, and possibly into inter-stellar space. But I must confess that I am a bit of a stick-in-the-muddy earth myself. My final judgement is, the slower, the better! Let me tell you why!

The last time our forebears took too big a bite at knowledge, they were expelled from the Garden of Eden. Adam was told he would henceforth eat only by the sweat of his brow, and Eve that she would in sorrow bring forth children.

This century of humankind has, for the first time, the chance to overcome this divine punishment by using knowledge of earthly tasks, like feeding the hungry, healing the sick and taking the sweat and agony out of human labour. We are in a position to transform the earth into which our ancestors were banished into a warm and gracious home for all their children.

Instead, this new great bite at knowledge that we are now contemplating, threatens our future in this other Eden into which we could turn the earth. Obviously only a few of us will ever be cosmonauts; but we must not underrate the impact which the space age may have on the human culture that earthbound man so painfully created. Many factual, intellectual, ethical and religious signposts, by which men in all their variety have learned to live, may become broken or obscured; we shall have to learn to live and think in time-space dimensions which, for most people, are still only theories in books, if they have heard of them at all.

Even the idiom of religious worship may have to adjust itself for while, logically, our entry into space does not disprove that there is a heaven, many people who now think there is a heaven may jump to the conclusion that it is disproved. Past thinkers have expressed their deepest awareness of realities in philosophical systems that we have called cosmologies. Oddly enough, once man actually moves out into the cosmos, all the cosmologies will become vulnerable to being overturned.

Ordinary earth dwellers, despite the grandeur of the cosmonauts, may come to feel that earth is a parish-pump rather than a lovely dwelling; that individual human life is trivial compared to the vistas of space. And the billions and billions spent on space adventures will encourage them to think so. I am afraid I have to be truthful, especially in this session on science and, frankly, despite the promised wonders of weather prediction and telecommunications, I would prefer, rather than face the wider implications of the race for space, to take the Sydney weather bureau at its worst, and send my message by smoke signals.

ANZUS Council on Indonesia and Holland; Aid to South Vietnam, the Common Market and Trade Deals

Thursday 10 May 1962, Notes on the News, 1.15pm 2BL

The communiqué issued by the ANZUS Council tell us less than we were already told before and during its meeting. Sir Garfield Barwick stressed that the ANZUS pact covered Australian Papua and New Guinea, and Mr Rusk[1] told the press that Australia 'can expect complete solidarity from the US on Australia's and New Zealand's responsibilities in the Pacific'. The communiqué confirms that ANZUS' mutual assistance obligations cover the parties' island territories.

Second, Mr Rusk said that the United States would do its best to ensure that the arms build-up in Indonesia would not be used in any 'improper way'. And the communiqué does the decent thing of expressing concern at threats of force in the area.

Third, Mr Rusk wanted Indonesia and Holland to come to a peaceful settlement, and the communiqué appeals to the parties to co-operate in U Thant's mediating efforts.

Fourth, he thought the interests and self-determination of the Papuans in West New Guinea were important to the UN and should be 'adequately taken care of'.

Military aid to South Vietnam was also discussed, and so was the European Common Market problem. The communiqué is silent as to this latter, but Dean Rusk, at his press conference, read a prepared statement on the US attitude to the question of Britain's entry.

On the Common Market, Mr Rusk frankly referred to the longstanding US campaign against 'trade restrictions of all sorts', including Commonwealth preferences. But he was less than frank in not referring to the equally longstanding US tariff policies resulting from the work of strong lobbies in Congress, which have hindered imports to the United States.

As consolation prizes for Australia, Mr Rusk hinted at possible long-term arrangements to bring order into the marketing of primary products, and at possible tariff reductions resulting from US negotiations with the European Common Market. Certainly, we could do with more considerate US policies both on tariffs and on agricultural surpluses.

But there is also involved, in all this, another steady American policy, which troubles me even more.

---

1   Dean Rusk, US Secretary of State 1961–1969.

Eleven years ago, Britain was deliberately excluded from ANZUS; and 10 years ago, even her request to send observers to the ANZUS conference at Honolulu was rejected. I remember saying to you at that time that I attached a different importance to the American attitude that led to this, from what was publicly stated at the time. After all, Britain was and is still a Pacific naval power, with as much or as little interest in the ANZUS area as the United States itself. The fact that British naval power alone no longer sufficed to protect Australia and New Zealand was no reason for cold-shouldering her altogether. America's attitude over the ANZUS Treaty (I said) could not be separated from her attitude to Europe. In Europe, consistent American pressure has been brought to commit Britain irrevocably to the European continent.

That pressure Britain long resisted because, among other things, she still could see her future only in close oceanic links with the Commonwealth and with the United States itself, and not as a mere insular appendage of continental Europe.

Britain's position may now have been changed on the economic side by the apparent success of the Common Market. But Britain still realises, as well as we do, that all the bonds of Britain with the Commonwealth will come into jeopardy if she enters the Common Market without due safeguards for the Dominion economies.

Taking a historical perspective, US attitudes at this 1962 ANZUS meeting seem to me to be unpleasantly continuous with those of the 1952 conference. In 1952, the US posted (as it were) a 'Keep Out' notice against Britain on the gates of ANZUS in the Pacific. In 1962 she is, somewhat more quietly, helping to post a 'Keep Out' notice against Australia and New Zealand at the gates of European Common Market, in which American policies are also deeply involved.

Mr Rusk, I am sure, has nothing but friendship for Britain and us. He is only pressing a longstanding American policy designed to pry Britain away from the Commonwealth and solidify her with Europe. But I regret that Washington is still doing this without adequate attention to its implications either for Britain, or Australia and New Zealand, or for the Commonwealth as a whole.

I doubt whether either Mr Rusk or the communiqué will quiet Australian unrest about Washington's policy on the West New Guinea issue. What can he mean by saying that Washington will do its best to see that the arms build-up in Indonesia will not be improperly used? Is Washington expecting Dutch forces to attack Indonesia? Does Washington support President Soekarno's demand of yesterday that Canberra should try to stop the Dutch reinforcing in West New Guinea? Altogether, Washington's attitudes to The Hague and Djakarta and to the possible role of the United Nations, are even stranger than Canberra's. After all, Washington should be providing leadership, not conducting international 'give away' sessions.

The ANZUS Treaty obligation in case of Indonesian attack on Australian New Guinea is not quite as explicit as many people think. Each party undertakes to treat an armed attack on any other in the Pacific as 'dangerous to its own peace and security', and to act 'to meet the common danger'.

But impressive as this sounds, it would not strictly oblige Washington to help defend Australian New Guinea in a military sense, This ANZUS article is much weaker than the corresponding NATO article, which says that an armed attack on one party is to be treated as an attack on all.

So when Mr Rusk promises complete solidarity from the US on Australia's and New Zealand's responsibilities in the Pacific, Washington would, in an emergency, still have a lot to keep talking about, for instance as to what Australian 'responsibilities' are in New Guinea, as well as about what Washington prepared to do about them.

It would be better, in my view, if Washington gave more thought to preventing such emergencies from arising.

Australia's Foreign Minister in Indonesia; Free Speech in the USA

Saturday 12 May 1962, Notes on the News

As he passed through Sydney on his return from Indonesia, Minister of Defence Townley[1] hit out at his critics who (he said) were speaking 'arrant nonsense' and expressing a 'most childish point of view'.

He explained that, on his tour, his good Australian shoes and suit were getting spattered with Indonesian mud, and that the Indonesian army camp commander courteously offered him jungle green and army boots. So he agreed (he said) 'to let the army tailor knock me up a pair of trousers and a Palm Beach shirt', and pinned his service ribbons onto this Indonesian version of a Palm Beach shirt.

All this was by way of denying a headline report from Djakarta on Sunday, that, while watching troops of the crack Indonesian Siliwangi Division, he adorned his Siliwangi uniform with his service ribbons.

Now I have no doubt that the men of the Siliwangi Division were also dressed in trousers and shirts 'knocked up' (in the Minister's eloquent words) by Indonesian army tailors. They certainly were not wearing the double-breasted civilian suits to which Deputy Prime Minister McEwen and I are addicted.

So it adds up to this: Mr Townley indignantly denied wearing his service ribbons on an Indonesian army uniform; and to prove his denial he explained that he first put on the uniform and then attached his ribbons. That seems an admission rather than a denial.

This, of course, is rather unfair to the minister. What he really meant is that while he did wear his ribbons on an Indonesian uniform, he did not intend to produce public and diplomatic repercussions in Australia, and in the capitals of the world.

But this leaves me still with a problem. I accept that Mr Townley did not intend to send around the world's capitals, at a time when the Indonesian army was openly using military force to try and seize West New Guinea, the picture of our Army Minister inspecting the Siliwangi Division, in what must have looked uncommonly like a Siliwangi uniform. I assume, therefore, that he did not intend to give backhand Australian support to Indonesia's use of force.

---

1   Athol Gordon Townley (3 October 1905 – 24 December 1963).

But a responsible minister should surely have known that this would be the effect; he should even have preferred to get some Indonesian mud on his Australian suit and boots, rather than let mud be spattered on the wisdom of the good name of Australia.

Even this may be rather charitable. No doubt Mr Townley had his duties as President Soekarno's guest. But these could not include treating the Australian public as fools. As a guest, no doubt, it was courteous for him to tell us of his 'most extraordinary welcome', though an ordinary one would have done in the circumstance.

No doubt, also, it is true, as he reminded us, that Perth is closer to Djakarta than to Sydney. But how this proves his point that we shouldn't worry about East New Guinea when Indonesia takes West New Guinea, I don't know. Can the minister mean that it is already too late to worry about our rights in New Guinea, and that we should begin worrying about Perth?

And then, how are we to understand Mr Townley's bland statement that his Indonesian hosts were 'too courteous to raise the question of West New Guinea'. Mr Townley's visit, as I understand it, was a return visit for that of General Nasution here. General Nasution had no guest-like scruples about getting Mr Menzies to promise to accept any West New Guinea settlement, which Indonesian pressure, short of force, could impose on the Dutch. Nor did General Nasution hesitate to go back within a year on his reciprocal promise not to use force.

Whatever his Indonesian hosts did, therefore, for the Army Minister to go to Djakarta at this moment, without raising the West New Guinea question was at least grossly imprudent. For his silence on it was an act of foreign policy more eloquent than any words.

United States Supreme Court Justice Black has flatly asserted that the guarantee of free speech under the First Amendment of the United States Constitution is so absolute as to forbid any legal restraint, even on defamatory or obscene matter, and even (he implied) to forbid restraints to protect national security.

Justice Black is well known as the leader of the so-called 'bleeding heart' minority of Supreme Court justices. They have waged a campaign, with considerable success, to strengthen the personal civil liberties guarantees of the Bill of Rights of the American Constitution.

American courts, at the moment, certainly do not accept Justice Black's view; they grant damages or injunctions for libels, just as our courts do, and read the guarantee of free speech subject to the police power of the state. For these remedies are based on the tradition of common law, and the free speech guarantee of the First Amendment is aimed rather against statutes passed by the Congress. Another legal complication is that, because of another amendment (the 14th), many, if not all, of the Supreme Court justices now interpret the Constitution in a way to extend the free speech guarantee even against statutes of the several states.

And in case you think you now understand the American constitutional position I ought to add that how the Supreme Court justices vote on particular civil liberties questions is rather unpredictable. Guessing how the Supreme Court will vote would give wonderful scope for starting price betting.

The French Army, de Gaulle and the Question of Algeria

Tuesday 29 May 1962, News Commentary, 2BL

The bewilderment among Frenchmen generally, and reportedly in the French cabinet itself, caused by the contrast between the High Military Tribunal's death sentence on General Jouhaud, and the mere imprisonment of his superior Salan, still dominates the French crisis. De Gaulle yesterday abolished the Tribunal, specially created to try high officers after the army revolt in 1961. Jouhaud has a temporary reprieve. The possibility of a new trial of Salan based on a new charge is being mooted.

Meanwhile, in Algeria, the illegal OAS army[1] is stepping up its scorched earth activity, and is threatening to use a new secret weapon, and the French political parties, including the newly legalised Muslim rebel party, are preparing for the referendum on the exact form of Algeria's future relations with France.

The chaos and violence of the Algerian issue are compounded of numerous elements.

In the background, first, are the difficulties that France has always had in achieving stable government under its multiple party system. De Gaulle came to emergency power in an effort, sponsored by the army, to rescue the Algerian question from the endless confusions and vacillations of French domestic politics.

Second, a foreground issue is the pressure of a million and a quarter European settlers in Algeria, the so-called *colons*, many of them settled there for more than a century, whose votes count in the Paris Chambers. Settler leadership has for decades fanatically pursued two objectives as critical for settler survival – to remain political master over the Muslims, and to maintain the close bond with France on which they depend economically and politically.

Third is the changing perspective of de Gaulle's foreign policy, and particularly its shift from overseas concerns like Algeria, towards Franco-German leadership in Europe.

Fourth, there is the leadership of the French army, not just of the army in Algeria or of the illegal OAS. For it is well to remember that Generals Jouhaud and Salan were condemned to death in their absence as long ago as 1961, for participation in the revolt in the high army command in that year.

---

1   *Organisation de l'armée secrete*, a dissident and secret paramilitary organisation formed during the Algerian War, dedicated to maintaining French dominance in Algeria.

It became clear at their 1961 trials that the officers, then charged and convicted, regarded themselves as justified in their action because of de Gaulle's policy, and that even their high colleagues, who were not implicated, regarded the rebellion with indulgence. General Gambiez, the Algerian Commander-in-Chief, himself pleaded for acquittal. 'Rendez-moi mes enfants', he cried, 'Give me back my children.'

From the army command's point of view, they had helped bring de Gaulle to power precisely to stop the rot of French authority in Algeria, but his policy since then had been incomprehensible to them. For 16 months he commanded them to fight and weaken the Algerian rebel (FLN).[2] Then in 1959 he proposed Algerian self-determination. This worried them enough. Then in 1960 he proposed and now persists in offering Algeria complete independence.

De Gaulle, in short, put his policy over piece by piece, without explaining it as a whole. No doubt there were good political reasons for this, but the effect on the military was well described by Colonel Guiraud, commanding one of the crack regiments, who was not implicated in the rebellion. 'My men', he said at the trials, 'did not know what they were fighting for any more. They were ready to die but they were torn apart by these shifts in policy.'

Soldiers of course, cannot be allowed to dictate foreign policy but soldiers are only human, and like to understand what they are ordered to risk their lives for, especially when today's order contradicts yesterday's. The confusions of the recent trials are a measure mainly of the cloud of unclarity that still hovers between the government of France and its army.

---

2   Front de Libération Nationale.

State Aid for Religious Schools – the Constitutional Issues

Tuesday 26 June 1962, Notes on the News

Yesterday, as if by way of commentary on current Australian controversies, the Supreme Court of the United States handed down an important decision on religious freedom and the separation of church and state. They held it unconstitutional for state authorities to require children in public schools to recite officially laid down prayers as a daily school exercise. Such prayers, they said, violated the guarantee of religious freedom in the First Amendment to the United States Constitution.

The principle underlying religious liberty, earlier American judges have said, means that the state should keep its hands off religions, and that religions should keep their hands off the state. Only thus, they have thought, could religious controversy be kept down in public life, and a struggle be avoided for the control of public policy and the public purse.

In earlier decisions, the court had held in 1943, on the application of the Jehovah's Witnesses sect, that it was unconstitutional for a state to require a compulsory flag salute as a regular part of public school activities and, in 1948, that it was also unconstitutional for the school authorities to set aside a weekly period for a right of entry by teachers sent by religious sects, even when the whole arrangement was approved and managed by the state school superintendent. They held that this was a use of public school buildings and machinery to aid sectarian groups. On the other hand, they had held it quite lawful for the state to provide free schoolbooks to all children, in both public and religious schools, and in effect to pay for the school transport for all such children.

The First Amendment to the US Constitution, under which yesterday's decision was made, reads simply that 'Congress shall make no law respecting an establishment of religion'. Our own Australian Constitution, in s.116, also forbids the Commonwealth to make any law for the establishment of religion.

Two questions will occur to you. One is how it comes about that, though the First Amendment to the US Constitution forbids only the federal Congress to establish a religion, yesterday's decision applied to all the several states. The brief answer is that another of the American guarantees, the Fourteenth Amendment (the 'due process clause') protects individual liberty in general, and does so against the states as well. The Supreme Court has held for a long time now that the religious guarantee of the First Amendment is a fundamental part of liberty, and therefore binds the states as well.

The next question you may ask is whether Australian constitutional law would come to the same result. The answer is, of course, yes! as regards any federal statute. But, as regards a state statute that tried to establish a religion or to set religious exercise in public schools, the answer is probably that it would not be unconstitutional. For our constitution arguably contains no clause like the due process clause of the US Constitution, through which the religious guarantee extends to the several states indirectly.

But the legal aspect is not of course the whole story. The political principle underlying yesterday's American decision is that religious freedom, and the non-establishment even of a common core, non-sectarian religion, are so fundamental to liberty, that they must be implied in the general liberty which is guaranteed against state as well as federal power.

I share the concern of many churchmen and other thoughtful people about the weakening of the influence of the family and of organised religion in the religious training of the young. But as we look desperately around for remedies, we should remember what may become involved if we choose the easy course of trying to use the state for this purpose.

The principle underlying religious liberty, earlier American judges have said, means that the state should keep its hands off religions, and that religions should keep their hands off the state. Only thus, they have thought, could religious controversy be kept down in public life, and a struggle be avoided for the control of public policy and the public purse. That may be an even more important principle to chew on, than a principle of law.

State Aid for Private Schools – Crisis and Analysis; Historic Joint Parade of French and West German Armies

Wednesday 11 July 1962, Notes on the News, 1.15pm 2BL

When, a fortnight ago, the United States Supreme Court struck down a New York law requiring teachers to lead a daily prayer exercise in the public schools, it was not really holding that prayer was unconstitutional. The thing that was unconstitutional was for the state to prescribe a prayer and require teachers to recite it in public schools.

This kind of distinction must always be remembered, whether we are arguing about religious instruction in public schools, or state aid to religious schools. Yesterday the Catholic school authorities in Goulburn, supported by a meeting of 500 parents and affecting more than 2,000 children, decided to close all their schools for six weeks in the very middle of the school year, in order to show their 'bitter disappointment' at their failure to get state financial aid. This startled the political leaders of the state into a deep silence, and the leaders of other denominations into hostile and even acrimonious criticism, in which harsh words like 'blackmail' are even being thrown about.

All this is a regrettable but salutary reminder of the reason why so many democratic states observe the principle of separation of church and state. The reason is to keep bitter religious controversy out of public life, by denying to every denomination any advantage from getting control of public policy or the public purse.

As many of us as possible should, I think, try to look calmly at the principles involved, free of sectarian passion. Here are some of the principles, as they appear to me.

1. Every child in the state is entitled to be educated in the public schools at public expense.

2. Therefore, the parent of any child in any private school, religious or other, is entitled to decide that he wants his child to leave the private school and attend the appropriate public school.

3. This right of parents is surely, however, subject to two conditions. First, it should be exercised at an appropriate time for admission of pupils so that the state education authority can make the necessary arrangements; second, it must be exercised for the education of the child at the public school, and not for ulterior motives of embarrassing the state educational authorities.

On the question of what aid can be given to religious schools consistent with separation of church and state, certain things are, in my opinion, clear and certain other things are very debatable, even among intelligent and reasonable citizens.

At one extreme, state aid for teachers' salaries in religious schools seems clearly inconsistent with the principle of separation of church and state, just as, according to the Supreme Court, is any state requirement that public school teachers should lead religious prayers. At the other extreme, it seems unobjectionable for the state to reimburse the parents of all school children, at whatever school, for the kind of education expenses common to them all – for instance, costs of travel to school, of secular textbooks, of patrolmen at school pedestrian crossings. In between, and debatable, despite the federal government's contributions of interest payments for private school buildings in Canberra, are the provision of school buildings, of meals, or of medical or public health services, or even sanitary services, within religious schools.

But here we are getting very near the immediate complaint of the Goulburn Catholic schools, that they can't afford to meet the Education Department's standards of lavatory accommodation. I hope I have said enough to indicate that such matters should be discussed only on a cool and salubrious level of debate.

The joint parade of French and West German forces on the field of Rheims, inspected jointly by Chancellor Adenauer and General de Gaulle, was undoubtedly historic, not only in this state visit, or in the history of the Cold War, but in all the sweep of modern world history, since Napoleon conquered and set up his puppets in Germany more than a century and a half ago.

Clearly, at the moment, France and West Germany are nearer to union than anyone was entitled to regard as conceivable in 1945. Economic union, led by France and West Germany is already in sight. Yet political union is still rather far off, even though the main outcome of Adenauer's visit is said to be an agreement to resume talks for political union among 'the Six' at Rome, in October.

For de Gaulle has always been opposed to the idea of merger into one supra-national state. He publicly ridiculed the idea less than seven weeks ago. He wants just a Paris-Bonn axis – or perhaps a Paris-Bonn-Rome axis. But a Paris-Bonn axis doesn't attract Italy; and other members of the Six oppose the inclusion of Italy in an axis with France and West Germany

Since the six Common Market countries are thus still vastly unclear about their common political future, we are entitled to be no less vastly puzzled about the many British declarations to the effect that it is the prospective political developments out of the Common Market which make it imperative for Britain to secure admission.

Walter Lippman, after his talk with de Gaulle, thought the General was cool towards Britain's entry into a common market because he feared Britain's political role in Europe. But this, I would suggest, is not because a United States of Western Europe is around the corner, but rather because the United States of America is at the front door. De Gaulle may well think that Britain's intimate presence would complicate the plans of the 'two old men' to save Europe for the Europeans, without actually losing their American friends.

Let Sleeping Dogs Lie – the Politics of Separation of Church and State

Monday 23 July 1962, News Commentary, 6.55 pm 2BL

Just a week ago Goulburn public schools admitted by a commendable emergency effort over 640 of the 2,200 children affected by the six weeks strike of Catholic schools, called the week before to protest against lack of state financial aid. Last night, obviously after careful assessment of public reactions to the strike, a further Goulburn meeting, by an overwhelming vote of 800 to 100, ended the Catholic school 'strike'.

The keynote of this second gathering, already mooted by spokesmen during the week, was that the 'strike' had now focused adequate attention on the needs of Catholic schools.

Yet, obviously, this is not very convincing. Even a week's school strike initiated by parents and clerical leaders is rare and dramatic enough to hit the headlines. Six weeks' closure was unnecessary for this purpose, or for that of bringing home what a great number of children attend Catholic schools, and how hard it is to fit them at short notice into the public schools.

If, on the other hand, the original purpose of fixing six weeks for the strike was to show how badly the public schools would be dislocated if all Catholic schools closed down suddenly, it had a boomerang effect. It led to lamentable charges of improper pressure on government and parliament – to words like 'blackmail' and 'children being used as a screen for a political campaigns'. And denials, however sincere, did not cancel these effects.

There was also another boomerang effect. The fact that feeling ran so very high must have led the NSW Premier Heffron and his ministers, whatever view they held on the issues, to maintain an impassive public countenance in face of the claims for aid. Mr Heffron said he wasn't going to be drawn into any 'sectarian fight'.

The bitter controversies have brought some gains. They have shown, for example, that aid to religious schools in the United Kingdom is on a basis of a degree of state control not likely to be acceptable in Goulburn. It has also become rather clear that solutions of the problem vary among different peoples according to the history and religious composition of each, making it rather risky for either side to pick a foreign example, out of context, to bolster its case.

In an earlier talk, I tried to trace some kind of a line between state aid that would and would not violate the principles involved. However you draw the line, it surely stops well short of the claim of last night's resolution that each religious denomination is entitled to receive out of the public treasury to spend on its own religious schools, an amount proportionate to the ratio of the number of children attending its schools, to the total children in the community.

Last night's meeting tried to reduce the issue to this, and to say that therefore it was one of justice, and not of sectarian rivalry, and it rebuked the NSW Premier for calling it a sectarian issue. On the same day, a speaker at a large Protestant gathering in Sydney declared that state aid would amount to state support for one religious group, would deepen 'the segregation pattern of Australian society', waste the scarce money available for education, lower educational standards and deepen the secularist nature of public schools by reducing the number of public school children coming from religious families.

Whichever side you take in such endless arguments, several points stand out. One of the most important is that a community where the dogs of religious strife are sleeping, should count itself happy, and that all sections of such a community should, if humanly possible, let the dogs lie sleeping. This, and not secularism, is the basic reason for the doctrine of separation of church from state. It is to prevent bitter and ever-recurring strife between religious groups for the control of public policy and the public purse.

Amid the lessons of the hates, fears and suspicions of the last fortnight, this wisdom, at least, should commend itself to all faiths and to the community as a whole.

Free Speech in Britain and South Africa

Thursday 9 August 1962, Notes on the News, 1.15pm 2BL

The entry of American Nazi demagogue Rockwell into England, to bring his message of race hatred to the tiny but vicious British National Socialist Movement, reminds us again what absurdities British constitutionalism sometimes gets into. Despite the fact that Rockwell had been forbidden entry to the UK, he came in easily and apparently under his own name, by landing first at Shannon in Ireland. Since the recent British Immigration Act, all Australians are documented and checked for entry into Britain. Australia has never had an anti-British rebellion, and Australia has never even tried to leave the Commonwealth. Even if you believe these events in Ireland were justifiable and even inevitable, it is still very strange that Nazi aliens can enter Britain from Ireland without the same checks as are now imposed on British subjects who are Australian.

The total membership of Nazi groups in Britain now trying to break into the news is about 200; with somewhat more allegedly in Scotland. Of course, democracy values free speech supremely; it does so because, by discussion, ideas can be thrashed out and the truth can become clearer. But the democracies should have learned enough about Nazi and other totalitarian methods, to know that not all words issuing from the mouth are speech or entitled to the privileges of free speech. When race psychopaths pour out a torrent of foul epithets accusing some section of the community of being rapists, filthy scum, and so on, this is not speech at all. It is neither offered nor received for discussion and clarification of truth. It is a verbal criminal assault and is so received by the listeners as well as the threatened victims.

The villagers of Dead and Bury Hollow in Gloucestershire who objected to their quiet valley being defiled by this verbal violence took the law into their own hands and ejected the small Nazi groups. Obviously, on principle, the prevention of such verbal violence and jack booting is the responsibility of a democratic parliament and government, and the *English Daily Herald* was therefore right to call on the British government to face its responsibilities.

The capture of Black Pimpernel Nelson Mandela by the South African government, leader of the now banned organisation for native equality in Africa, marks a stage in the deepening South African tragedy. It was announced the same day as an important South

African project in zoology. A report from Pretoria, the federal capital, tells us that the liaison officer of the South African National Parks Board is planning to learn the languages of animals and birds, so that human beings will be able to communicate with them. It is only a month or two, you may recall, since South Africa enacted a new repressive public security act, which turns into treason with dire penalties, a great range of speech between human beings.

We should not therefore, really be surprised at the new search for ways of talking to animals and birds, for so many South Africans do really need birds and animals to talk to. And they may think anyhow that animal and bird language is safer these days.

What is surprising is that a South African government official should have dared to mention in public so obvious a manoeuvre to evade the new law of treason. So far, the government has done nothing. But Dr Verwoerd is bound before long to tumble to what it means. When he does, we can be sure that the new treason law will be extended to cover the intimate conversations between Nobel Prize winner Chief Luthuli and the birds and animals of South Africa.

UK Neo-Nazis on Trial; US Proposal for Atom Test Bans; A Comment on President Nasser

Thursday 30 August 1962, Notes on the News, 1.15pm 2BL

Members of the tiny Nazi movement in England, including its ex-schoolmaster Führer Colin Jordan, are before a London court charged with participating in a quasi-military organisation, contrary to the Public Order Act of 1936. This prosecution is a sequel to the secret Nazi training camp of a few weeks ago, at a quiet beauty spot near Cheltenham in Gloucestershire, with the wonderful name, Dead and Bury Hollow.

According to police evidence thus far, it seems that training a private military organisation is one of their fantastic activities. Apparently, the men charged are a part of a small, self-styled elite of this several hundred strong Nazi Party, who are deliberately copying Hitler's infamous storm troopers of the 1930s.

They are apparently training themselves and their supporters in straight Hitlerite doctrine, as well as in its vilest practices. Equipment seized at their London headquarters included, among other items, tins of poison with instructions as to use, which make clear that members of the movement are being trained and psychologically conditioned to use poison gas for mass murder of such of their fellow human beings as they wish to be rid of.

I can well understand that the British government takes this business seriously. There was a time when Hitler and his storm troopers also were counted only in hundreds, and met in small secret conclaves singing 'Horst Wessel' and yelling 'Heil Hitler' in the beer-gardens of Munich. But within the next 20 years this group of madmen was governing the Third Reich, had started a great world war, costing millions of soldiers' lives, and massacred in cold blood, more than six million men, women and children.

Tins of mock poison gas, with training instructions for use in gas chambers, may seem childish things. But in Hitler's Auschwitz extermination camp from 1942 to 1944, Nazi figures show that two and a half million men, women and children were murdered by psychopaths and sadists who had learned simple instructions on how to drive people into gas chambers and set the poison gas hissing. The two and a half million gassed at Auschwitz were less than half of those murdered in all the Nazi camps.

Clearly, democratic peoples may and must protect themselves not only against paramilitary training of dangerous lunatics, but also against instigation of them to mass murder of their fellow human beings. It is a grave offence to incite another individual to murder even a single victim. Why should it not be at least an equally grave offence to incite

99

to the murder of hundreds of thousands? On no sensible interpretation of political liberty is this a part of it.

The new Western draft for a nuclear test ban, which President Kennedy hoped yesterday would bring a nuclear test ban by 1 January next, was presented at Geneva on Tuesday, and offers two alternatives. The first would ban all tests, whether in the atmosphere, in space or underground. As to the atmosphere and space, the new draft omits the provisions for inspection and policing on which Western states have up to now insisted, and which Moscow has rejected as a mere cover for espionage. But as to underground tests, this first alternative draft still insists on provisions for on-the-spot inspection.

The point is that each side can already detect, with instruments it already has at home, explosions made by each, both above and below ground. But as to underground tests, no instruments are yet available which can, at such a distance, distinguish nuclear tests from natural earth tremors.

Soviet representative Kuznetsov's immediate answer to this first draft was to stand pat on opposition to any local inspection, even if limited to underground tests.

No doubt expecting this, the Western powers had also offered a second alternative, a more limited plan to ban all tests above ground, leaving underground testing unaffected. Moscow may take this second more limited proposal seriously. And if anything came of it, this would be a real advance, not only as a beginning for the wider ban, but also because underground tests have the smallest side effects by way of radiation poisoning of the world's air and land.

That still leaves the question why, at the present stage, the West could not afford to abandon its pressure for on-the-spot inspection even for underground tests. If Moscow refused such a plan, its propaganda complaints about fearing espionage would be revealed as hypocrisy. If it accepted, this would be one step forward.

Of course, there would be a risk that Moscow would violate the agreement by secret underground testing. But, in any case, as things are now, both states do what they want, anyhow. And according to some reports, even underground tests may become detectable by the other side's instruments in the near future.

I recently said that the world's good wishes for the Nasser regime's tenth anniversary should include the earnest wish that President Nasser might turn to wiser and more peaceful policies towards his fellow Arab, as well as his Israeli neighbours. Some commentators came to the defence of Nasser with an emphatic 'I believe'. Even while they were talking, there were reports of Nasser stirring up further disorders among his Arab neighbours, and of further threats of aggression against Israel. And some of this came out into the open at yesterday's meeting of the Arab League. In face of Syria's charges, Nasser's answer was to instruct his delegate to walk out.

Everyone knows, of course, that 'I believe' is no substitute for knowing. And there I must leave it.

Comments on Capital Punishment; The Future of New Guinea

The clergyman son of the poor woman murdered by Tait[1] in Victoria is among those agitating for the murderer's reprieve and the abolition of the death penalty in that state. On the other hand, Presbyterian minister McEwen offered in his capacity as a citizen (not, he stressed as a clergyman) to perform the execution himself if the government could not find anyone else to do the job.

We must not, of course, confuse this Mr McEwen with the Deputy Prime Minister McEwen. The Deputy Prime Minister can be bloodthirsty enough, it is true, but I doubt whether he would come at hanging, or rather, if he did, it would be of other people, outside Australia.

What interests me in the Rev. McEwen's offer is the basis he gives for it. In effect, he says, he believes in his Bible, and the Bible says blood for blood, life for life, eye for an eye, and so on. There is a widespread belief that these phrases, which do undoubtedly appear in the Bible, represent a divine command that we shall thus relentlessly seek retaliation in kind and quantity for wrong done. Now I am not, of course, a theologian able to argue theology with the Rev McEwen. But I know a little about law and the history of law. And I do know that his interpretation of the biblical words is regarded as probably incorrect, both for when they were laid down, and for today.

Rules like 'an eye for an eye, a tooth for a tooth' were laid down for primitive tribes whose members still practised the blood feud and private vengeance generally. The blood feud was as likely to exact a life for an eye, and ten lives for one, and to lead to an endless chain of suffering. The legislator's purpose was to limit man's cruelty to man, not to insist on it. An eye for an eye, not two eyes for one eye, and not a life for an eye. It was, in other words, to stop excess of vengeance, not to insist on vengeance. It was to forbid gratuitous infliction of suffering, not to insist on the infliction of suffering regardless of the rational purpose this may serve.

The question of abolition of capital punishment is, of course, a difficult one, that I can't deal with today, but so is the question, what should be done with convicted murderer Tait.

---

1   Robert Peter Tait was convicted of murder in 1961 and sentenced to death.

While Canberra denies that it is under UN pressure to grant full self-government to Australian Papua-New Guinea by 1964, reports now circulating indicate that the date 1969 is being canvassed and wise steps are being taken by the Legislative Council to test out the opinions of the inhabitants themselves.

The Indonesian move into West New Guinea has made these and other problems also rather acute. One immediate problem was highlighted last night at a Sydney meeting of an association called ' Amnesty', whose headquarters are in London.

This association does good work to keep our consciences alive to the plight of thousands of unfortunates in many countries who have been imprisoned for reasons of conscience and politics, usually without a trial and often without being even charged with any offence.

Last night's meeting adopted a resolution entreating both the Australian and Indonesian governments to allow permanent residents on each side of their common frontier in New Guinea, to transfer their permanent domicile if they wished to, to the other side of the frontier. There is a sensible proviso that individuals who thus opt to change, should thereafter not meddle in the internal affairs of the country they have abandoned.

Obviously, the main hardships which the proposal aims to forestall are those of persons in Dutch New Guinea who might be in the black books of Djakarta because of their hostility to the Indonesian invasion. The proposal is, I think, both a humane and prudent one, and I hope it is taken seriously both in Canberra and Djakarta.

Nuclear Disarmament, Nuclear Tests

Tuesday 11 September 1962, Notes on the News, 1.15pm 2BL

Both Sir Garfield Barwick and Deputy Opposition Leader Whitlam made statements about nuclear disarmament at the weekend, and nuclear test bans have been recently in the news, so it may be as well to sort things out a little in this confusing area.

Three different aspects of the nuclear threat are involved. First, the test ban negotiations in Geneva are an attempt to stop new weapons testing and a preliminary step to nuclear disarmament. These negotiations are now waiting for Moscow's reply to an important US proposal for banning all except underground tests, without any on-the-spot inspections.

Second is the problem of general and nuclear disarmament itself, on which there has been a long weary series of statements and conferences since 1946, of which the latest opened in March last, at the urging of the last General Assembly. At that 17-nation conference for the first time a dozen non-nuclear powers, including the most influential neutral states, sat with the nuclear powers, to see if their wisdom could break the stalemate. It didn't.

Sir Garfield's recent statement concerned a further appeal from the UN to its members as to whether an even bigger conference of UN members generally should now be called to try and ban nuclear weapons. He said Canberra thought not.

The third problem, which the Labor Opposition is pressing, is that of making the whole of the southern hemisphere a nuclear-free zone. And, of course, you can't wholly separate it from the general disarmament question.

The broad issue on which all disarmament talks keep breaking down is that the US claims that a treaty ban on nuclear weapons must be properly inspected and policed by independent personnel, otherwise it will be only a snare and a delusion; while Moscow says that inspection would be a cover for spying inside the Soviet Union. Canberra takes the US view on this, and also on the other main Washington-Moscow disagreement. This is that you cannot negotiate nuclear disarmament separately from conventional disarmament. Both sides, indeed, have now come to agree on this point, and both make high-sounding speeches about complete and universal disarmament. But the new UN conference now proposed would be on nuclear weapons only.

The obvious reason for the Western view is that the West would be put at the greatest disadvantage by a ban on nuclear weapons without limiting conventional weapons. Even now NATO forces are still well short of the minimal figure of 30 divisions set as a minimal target. And this is the central point behind President Kennedy's weekend request to Congress for authority to call up 150,000 reservists in case of need.

In any case, when the dozen neutralist states at the 17-nation conference in March produced no new constructive idea, there does indeed seem little point in having an even bigger one. Many heads may sometimes make wise counsel; but in this case, I think, the larger the crowd, the emptier the function.

The argument about a nuclear-free southern hemisphere is, I am afraid, rather a storm in a teacup. Nuclear weapons can now be delivered on target three or four thousand miles away. The US has just announced a nuclear submarine Polaris missile base at Guam in the northern hemisphere. If the Soviet Union or China established ICBM[1] bases or long-distance bomber bases in northern Sumatra or Borneo, also in the northern hemisphere, a ban in the southern hemisphere would not help anyone very much. Solutions, I'm afraid, are not as easy as that.

---

1   Inter-Continental Ballistic Missiles (ICBMs), that can travel over 5500 kilometres, were first developed in the 1950s by both the USA and the Soviet Union to deliver nuclear weapons, particularly hydrogen bombs.

Mississippi Challenges Federal Rulings on Civil Rights

Friday 5 October 1962, Australia Looks at the World

Since 1961, Americans have begun celebrating the hundred year anniversaries of their Civil War, which raged from 1861 to 1865, over the issue of slavery. These celebrations, and the world stature which the United States has attained, testify to Lincoln's Gettysburg vision that a great nation cannot survive half-slave and half free. Yet I doubt whether, even with his great vision, Abraham Lincoln could have seen how long and hard, for both white and black Americans, is the road to a truly free society.

Let us at the outset not mistake this crisis, over James Meredith's entrance into the all-white university at Oxford, Mississippi, for a simple question of white people demanding to dominate black people. Problems as grave are found between coloured peoples themselves.

It is already half a century and more since Mahatma Gandhi dedicated himself to emancipating the untouchables in India. He renamed them Harijans, or children of God, in the effort to re-educate his fellow Hindus. And it is already 15 years since the equal rights of the untouchables with other Indians were sanctified in the impressive Bill of Rights of the Indian Constitution. Yet, in the broad sweep of Indian social and cultural and political life, the untouchables are still largely where they have been for centuries, hemmed in by their fellow Hindus' walls of exclusion, prejudice and taboo, which law and the courts can barely touch. And the question – what can law and government do to change this situation, even gradually – remains one of Prime Minister Nehru's most heart-breaking problems.

We have to dismiss such oversimplifications to see the full context of this week's showdown in which State Governor Barnett, with his Lieutenant Governor Johnson, personally led the flouting of the Federal Court's order to admit Meredith to the University of Mississippi, and mobilised the state militia ostensibly to prevent violence against Meredith, but in reality to prevent the execution of the court's order by 25 US Marshals.

Some of this fuller context lies deep back in the origins of the American Union, when it was still a live and vital issue how far each state was to maintain its full sovereignty even against Washington. Even after the present Constitution was adopted, and quite apart altogether from the slavery issue, it was still argued in some of the Southern states that a state legislature might 'interpose' between federal laws and the state's own citizens. It was in 1800 that the Virginia and Kentucky governments tried in this way to block the federal alien and sedition laws. It is ironic to recall that this Southern stand was a liberal protest against repressive laws inherited from the struggle for independence.

Right until the great Chief Justice Marshall's judgement of 1803 in Marbury v. Madison, the question was in doubt – what was to happen when legislation, state or federal, violated the federal constitution? That case settled that the judge's power and duty were to strike down as void a law violating the constitution; and that the federal judges had the last say.

Even after this, and even down to the contemporary crisis over segregation, the right of state interposition has continued to be agitated in the Southern states. Only yesterday the Mississippi legislature solemnly resolved that Washington had violated the sovereignty of the State of Mississippi and Article 4 of the Federal Constitution, by sending its marshals and armed troops into Mississippi. It is true that in Article 4 Section 4, the federal government guarantees republicanism to the states and protects them against invasion. But Washington's answer will certainly be that this Article does not absolve the states from obedience to constitutional and federal law. At a pinch, a state's claim to defy this law could only be made good by secession; and one of the main issues settled by the fratricidal Civil War of a century ago was whether secession was to be allowed.

That Civil War not only settled that there was no right of secession, but also freed the slaves and gave them by law equal rights as citizens. But, as in modern India, legal emancipation was only the beginning of the struggle to substitute one social pattern for another. The Southern states, ever since, have fought obstinate and often ingenious rear-guard actions year by year, institution by institution, practice by practice, to preserve the older patterns of class privilege, and stem the tide of equality.

The black student James Meredith, as a war veteran, symbolises the spirit of equality observed in the US armed forces since World War II. Until the Brown case, known as the 'desegregation case', in 1954 the judicial decisions still tolerated 'separate but equal' treatment of whites and blacks. But courts became ever harder to convince that facilities could be equal, if they were separate. The Brown case squarely declared that separate facilities could not be equal enough, and ordered desegregation 'with all deliberate speed'.

Once the Supreme Court has the last word, and secession is impossible, you disobey the court on pain of jail for contempt, and you resist its officers on pain of punishment for sedition and even treason. Most Southern state leaders, including their lawyers and professional men, contrary to general impression, are probably not in their hearts passionately hostile to desegregation. They appear to be so in public because they have to bid for popular and client support; and they fear that if they try to re-educate their communities into desegregation, they will cease to be leaders overnight. This is why the Conference of State Governors in Florida, now taking place, has refused to censure Governor Barnett of Mississippi. For most Southern leaders, the escape from the cleft stick of federal power and local opinion is to be put under compulsion by federal court orders and a few US marshals, or as in Little Rock, by a brief show of military force. Once that is done, things settle down; and in most Southern states (including Arkansas) much progress has been made without even a threat of military force.

Mississippi is a harder nut to crack, however, for two reasons. One is that the whites are a small minority facing nearly 80 percent blacks. Only Alabama has a higher percentage of black people. In Mississippi, too, the pre-Civil War pattern of aristocracy and class stratification survives most fully. Its university (as the name Oxford implies), caters for sons and daughters of this aristocratic minority; the entry of the descendants of black slaves is felt to strike at the heart, if not the brain of the Mississippi white civilisation. The other big difference in Mississippi is that Governor Barnett, unlike most Southern leaders, is not just a political conformist in his hatred of desegregation; he hates it from fanatical personal conviction. Clearly wounds will take long to heal in Oxford, Mississippi, even now that open violence has ceased, The Department of Justice has just declared that federal marshals and troops will continue to guard James Meredith for the whole 18 months of his university course.

There is a general admiration for the firmness of President Kennedy's decisions in this week's crisis. But federal courts, marshals and soldiers are a slow and hazardous approach to remoulding such deeply ingrained social attitudes, and deeply felt threats to group survival and self-respect. Black leadership that may spring from the new opportunities, white leadership too among individuals and groups especially of the churches, and perhaps more Washington initiatives in educating both sides in the social problems of race relations may bring reconciliation in the long run. As James Meredith walked into the classroom on Friday for the first time unescorted, some students jeered, and most were silent. But there was one white student who said 'Hello' and Meredith smiled 'Hello' in reply.

Good luck to both of them!

And good afternoon to all of you.

Capital Punishment and the Value of Human Life

Tuesday 16 October 1962, News Commentary, 2FC

Of the views that are being agitated as to whether Victorian convicted murderer Robert Tait should be hanged, that of the Reverend Irving Benson of Wesley Church, Melbourne comes nearest my own. He opposes capital punishment, but dissociates himself from hysterical views, which breathe fire and brimstone against anyone who does not oppose Tait's execution.

> As a usual punishment in short, we should be able to dispense with capital punishment. In the words of the great reformer John Bright 'a deep reverence for human life is worth more than a thousand executions in the prevention of murder. It is, in fact, the great security of human life.'

Though Tait's insanity was an issue at the trial and has recently been raised again in relation to his impending execution, it is obvious that most of the leaders of churches, trade unions, universities, politicians and citizens, and 91 Victoria barristers who have spoken against Tait's execution are not primarily concerned about his sanity, or about the fact he had a bad fall as a boy, or his previous record of violence and parole from prison, followed by the terribly brutal murder for which he faces execution.

They are really protesting against the Victorian government's decision, for the first time in 11 and a half years, to allow a hanging for murder. The Reverend Alan Walker gave the keynote at Sydney's 1000 strong protest meeting last Sunday when he said, 'Punishment must be reformatory. Hanging is barbaric.' The issue, in short, is whether we should join a number of other democratic states in abolishing capital punishment.

On this issue, the cardinal principle seems to be that, in a civilised society, punishment of the criminal must stop short of denying his humanity. For a society to act in a way, which denies the humanity of the criminal, is to deny it to all of us. A society in which cruel and unusual punishments prevail is likely to be one in which life generally is treated as cheap and expendable.

Against this are urged principles of social protection and deterrence. But what is needed to protect society, and whether a given punishment deters, are questions of facts.

In reality, statistics do not appear to support the idea that abolition of capital punishment necessarily leads to an increase in the number of murders in general. As to deterrence, it appears to be the case that most murders are done either from impassioned impulse, against which no deterrent will help, or secretly in the expectation that the murderer or even the murder itself will escape discovery.

The social gains from capital punishment seem therefore questionable. The facts of our Australian situation also raise doubts whether any grave evils would follow abolition.

In all the Australian states, including both Victoria and New South Wales, there has for some years been an average of less than one execution a year. No major problems appear to have arisen as a consequence. No doubt, it is more expensive to imprison murderers for life than to put them to death. But this is rather a small price to pay for manifesting fully society's respect for the sanctity of human life. The main peril is of later release of dangerous prisoners on parole, and the Tait and Lawson cases indicate that the words 'Never to be released' should be taken far more seriously by the officials concerned than they sometimes have been.

I think also that we should not be fanatical about absolute abolition. Society, its officers and its individual members, are all entitled to defend themselves physically against physical attacks by whatever force is reasonable. There may also be cases, like the Eichmann case, where the proximity of tens of thousands of likely avengers of the victims of multiple crimes makes it simply impracticable to protect him for life in prison. But such cases, we may hope, would be the rarest exceptions. As a usual punishment in short, we should be able to dispense with capital punishment. In the words of the great reformer John Bright[1] 'a deep reverence for human life is worth more than a thousand executions in the prevention of murder. It is, in fact, the great security of human life.'

---

1   Presumably the British Parliamentarian John Bright (1811–1889).

Cuban Missile Crisis – the Need for a Political Solution

Wednesday 31 October 1962, News Commentary

The Khrushchev-Kennedy deal, which damped down the Cuban crisis this weekend, consisted of an exchange of promises – two for two. Khrushchev undertook that the missile bases already built or being built would be dismantled and withdrawn, and that no further offensive arms would be shipped to Cuba. Kennedy undertook in return not to bomb or invade Cuba, and once the dismantling of bases was completed, under UN supervision, to lift the blockade of Cuba.

So that today's news that the United States has lifted its arms blockade of Cuba for 48 hours must not be mistaken for the end of either the blockade or the crisis, though we may hope it is the end of its acutest phase. The lifting is a temporary gesture of encouragement to U Thant and his 30-man team who have now arrived in Cuba to supervise the promised dismantling.

Probably, too, it is intended to soothe the smart of Moscow's wounds after the humiliating experience of having to admit charges of offensive preparations in Cuba, the very day after Mr Khrushchev passionately denied them. And President Castro's position needs soothing too, for no one should fail to notice that Mr Khrushchev dealt with bases in Cuba as if they were Soviet rather than Cuban bases.

But I want to devote our few minutes tonight to the United States blockade itself, and in particular, its status under international law. Even many US sympathisers took it for granted last week that the blockade must be a violation of international law, because blockade is forbidden under the UN Charter.

On the first point, the answer is simple. Naval blockade in peace time, known as pacific blockade, was a procedure well known to international law throughout the 19th century, even for such minor purposes as compelling a state debtor to pay its debts. This, for example, was the way the Great Powers in 1827 compelled Turkey to liberate Greece, and there were over 20 pacific blockades in the following century. For the purpose of collecting debts, such blockade was declared illegal early in this century, but not for other purposes.

> A third … (justification for a naval blockade in peacetime) … is the general right of self-preservation of states, a right which exists both in peace and war. The point I am making is that people who are dogmatic about the legal rights and wrongs are either novices at international law, or are speaking from prejudice.

The second question, whether the UN Charter forbids blockade, is more complicated. My view would be that the Charter forbids its use by a single state to enforce a particular policy, demands for money, or territory or the like. But this is only the beginning of the question.

At least four grounds for legality of its blockade can still be argued by Washington.

One is that the blockade was endorsed by the Organisation of American States as a regional organisation under the Charter. The difficulty with this is that enforcement action taken by the organisation would need an authorisation by the Security Council.

A second is that, in any case, the blockade was a collective act of self-defence of members of the Organisation of American States licensed under Article 51 of the Charter. The poising of missiles deliverable within five minutes is (Washington could argue) equivalent to 'armed attack' under that Article.

A third is the general right of self-preservation of states, a right which exists both in peace and war.

The point I am making is that people who are dogmatic about the legal rights and wrongs are either novices at international law, or are speaking from prejudice. The final reality is that international law says nothing very clear about the kind of choice with which modern nuclear warfare confronts states. And, by the way, when you meet people who tell you how law-abiding on this matter Moscow is, please remind them from me that the pre-emptive nuclear attack is a Moscow idea, and that Mr Khrushchev himself has been known to threaten with nuclear attack, European states that allow American missile bases to be established on them.

Capital Punishment, Mercy Killings; Two Political Footnotes

Thursday 8 November 1962, Notes on the News

When the High Court comes finally to dispose of the appeals about the murderer Tait's insanity it will be its third attempt, in a confused course of events, which perhaps I may sort out for you.

The court's first attempt, in Melbourne eight days ago, was frustrated by the Victorian government's strange haste in fixing a date for Robert Tait's execution[1] only 24 hours ahead of the High Court's hearing of appeals from the Victorian Supreme Court decision given only the night before.

The High Court declined to do its important work under such unseemly pressure and stayed Tait's execution until it could hear properly prepared legal argument in Sydney on Tuesday this week, that is, Melbourne Cup Day.[2]

The day before the Melbourne Cup, the press reported that the Victorian government had commuted Tait's death sentence on the ground that the repeated postponements had disturbed his mental health. The haste to execute Tait last Thursday was probably due to the fact that, under the new provisions of the Victorian *Mental Health Act 1959*, s. 52, which were about to come into effect, his case would fall within the category of mental illness or intellectual defect requiring him to be removed to an institution as a security patient.

But when the High Court made its second effort to deal with the insanity appeals on the day after the commutation, it was again frustrated, this time by the Melbourne Cup event. For one of the major ways in which Victoria is a more advanced state than NSW, is that Cup Day is a public holiday.

When the five-judge court and a distinguished array of counsel assembled in Sydney on Tuesday, the court wanted to know of the Crown whether there was any reason to

---

1   Robert Peter Tait was convicted of murder in 1961 and sentenced to death. In 1962, an appeal was lodged for a stay of Tait's execution, on the grounds of insanity. In an atmosphere of intense public debate about capital punishment, the government of the state of Victoria argued strongly for Tait's execution. In the December after this talk, his death sentence was finally commuted, and his case was designated 'never to be released'. He died in jail, in 1984.
2   The Melbourne Cup is an iconic horse race, run on the first Tuesday of November.

continue with the appeals, and this depended on whether the commutation was just a temporary reprieve, or whether (in Justice Kitto's words) 'Tait will not be executed now whatever happens'. Counsel for the Crown Shaw formally admitted that he did not really know what the answer was. But for Melbourne Cup holiday, of course, Mr Shaw could have obtained a firm answer from Melbourne in half an hour. As it was, the High Court hearing had to be adjourned until adequate information became available of requisite official steps to notify the Victorian Supreme Court of the commutation under s. 497 of the Victorian *Crimes Act.*

If the High Court holds that the commutation bars Tait's execution in any event, it will then have to consider whether any purpose is to be served by continuing to hear the appeals about Tait's sanity under the law, apart from the new *Mental Health Act.*

A very different aspect of the murder problem, that of 'mercy killing', is now the centre of world attention in the trial in Brussels, Belgium of the tragic young mother of 25, Mme van der Put, along with her husband, sister, mother and doctor as alleged accomplices for the murder of her seven-day-old, hopelessly deformed ' thalidomide' baby. The Belgian position is rather like it was in Victoria before the Tait case, namely that while the death sentence can be imposed, it is virtually always commuted. Extenuating circumstances may, however, also reduce the sentence to a minimum of three years' imprisonment.

I suppose it is the mother's position and the doctor's position that raise the really momentous and piteous questions of the trial. Nursing Sister Philomena of the hospital where the child was born spoke for the present state of the law in Belgium and in British countries as well when, showing the pathetic child to its mother for the first time, she said 'It is God who gives life and God who takes away life'.

Yet, it is often not as simple as that for the doctor, and the medical line between not prolonging life and shortening it may be a very difficult one to draw, for example with cases of incurable pain-ridden diseases. This case, of course, does not involve that situation; it involves rather the human consequences of freak side effects of modern drugs. But, even then, one of the doctor-witnesses is alleged to have said about his baby, which (he said) could only live a year or two 'I will do nothing to cause it to die, nor anything to cause it to live.'

The sanctity of human life lies deep in all our religious and social traditions. But yesterday's showing in the Brussels court of pictures not only of limbless babies, but 'seal babies' with hands growing out of their shoulder, and other horrifying effects of thalidomide leaves many big question marks for the community and for parliament, apart from the terrible responsibility of the drug industry.

Yet children, even when they are sound in all respects, are always at the mercy of older people, and especially of their parents. Any community that thinks about reforming the law of homicide for such cases would also do well to remember that, according to recent British Home Office statistics, 75 percent of all child victims of murder in England in 1961 were killed by their own parents or older relatives.

Life is hard in so many senses, isn't it?

Let me conclude with one or two foreign affairs items. The resignation of the former Indian Defence Minister holds no wonder for anyone familiar with the Indian scene. The wonder has been how Krishna Menon could for so many years maintain high responsibilities in a country where practically no one in public life, except Prime Minister Nehru, trusts either his judgement or his devotion to Indian, as opposed to Moscow and communist interests.

One comment, finally, on the US elections, in which a third Kennedy brother has become a Senator. JFK used just to stand for President Kennedy's name; but wags are now saying it stands for 'Jobs for Kinsfolk', which of course is only a little better than 'Jobs for Kennedys'.

Asian Conflicts and Hypocrisy

Sunday 18 November 1962, Australia Looks at the World

The continuing Chinese attack[1] at Walong, the most massive so far, is at the Burmese end of India's north-east frontier. Tawang River, another main point of fighting, is at the Bhutan end. A third appears to be emerging further west, at Chumbi Valley, at the junction of Bhutan and Sikkim, and only 35 miles downhill to India's only railway junction with her northeast forces.

I keep thinking, as this crisis unfolds, of the first time Nehru publicly admitted its long-term gravity. It was at Sapru House, a think tank for the study of world affairs in New Delhi, in 1960. I thought he spoke like a prophet, but one publicly proclaiming how bad a prophet he had been in the past. India, he declared, must get used to the idea that her 2,500-mile northern frontier was now alive and would not settle down again in our times.

Geographically this frontier is the Himalayan 'roof of the world'. Politically it consists of one long frontier with Outer Tibet, with three main sectors. The middle sector, made up of the Indian-protected states, Bhutan, Sikkim and Nepal, bulges into the great North Ganges Indian plain towards Patna, Benares, Lucknow and Delhi. The north-east frontier sector runs eastward from the Bhutan end of the bulge to the Burma frontier on the east. The third, north-west sector is in the Lesser Himalayan and the Ladakh Range area, with Kashmir and the Pakistan frontier at one end of it, and Nepal at the other.

Most of the disputed areas were not too important until the growth of modern transport methods; and it is in the north-east sector that the ground of dispute is more specific. It concerns the validity of the boundary line known as the McMahon Line, drawn at the Simla Conference between British India, Tibet and China in 1914, but later repudiated by China.

Here the Chinese claim comprises most of the area of what is still known by the British name of North East Frontier Agency, an area still serving, as under the British, as a buffer zone, alongside Nepal, Sikkim and Bhutan, against Asian advance from the north. An enemy established here can readily sweep down the Brahmaputra valley on to the great fertile delta region of Bengal.

---

1   Part of the China-India War of 1962

Ostensibly, right along this disputed frontier, the rival claimant to Indian territory is the state of Tibet, that lofty, long-isolated, mystical and mysterious prototype of all Shangri-las.[1] In fact, the claimant is Communist China, which has imposed its will in Tibet.

It is of India, Tibet and China, and of Nehru's principles of anti-imperialism, neutralism, non-intervention and negotiation, that I want mainly to talk, today. For we should recognise that India's present crisis is not only a border crisis, not only a military crisis, but also a spiritual crisis and a crisis of political ideology.

The story of Tibet, as well as those of Kashmir and Goa, cast a cold revealing light on the way in which Asian as well as communist states all enunciate high-sounding principles against the West, which they are not willing to abide by themselves.

How does it come to be Communist China that is pressing the supposed territorial claims of Tibet? Briefly it is because Peking China, without any serious protest from India, virtually annexed Tibet in the mid-50s, and has since then built up her forces there to 14 divisions, or about 110,000 men. Nehru's India gave refuge to the Dalai Lama, but only on the condition that he refrained from political statements and activities challenging Chinese violations of the status of Tibet.

Within a year or so, Peking began publishing maps placing the North East Frontier Agency on the Chinese/Tibetan side of the border. Mao Tse-Tung and Chou En-Lai denounced what they called 'trespassing and provocation' by Indian troops, in September 1959, declared the McMahon frontier line to be a product of British aggression, and the Treaty of Simla to be an unequal treaty imposed by an imperialism, on which an anti-imperialist like Nehru should be ashamed to rely.

I am not saying, of course, that the Chinese are right about the frontier. When I was consulted in Delhi, my conclusions on the law honestly favoured the Indian case. But then I am not Mr Nehru. It is Mr Nehru who has steadily supported the overthrow of legal relations established by imperialist power, and accepted complacently the Communist Chinese absorption of Tibet. And the same Mr Nehru now finds India confronted with its deadliest threat, not from old-fashioned imperialists, but from a very modern Asian communist imperialism; and he addresses his main appeals for military support to Western capitals, which he has so often lectured on the evils of force and imperialism, and on the virtues of neutralism and compromise.

This crisis of spirit and political ideology is also obvious with the North West frontier area, adjacent to beautiful and bitterly disputed Kashmir. No less than half a million of India's trained soldiers are pinned down in Kashmir by the longstanding struggle with Pakistan for its possession.

Here again, I am not concerned with the rights and wrongs of the Kashmir dispute, but rather with the crisis in India's professed principles of policy, which accompany the present military crisis. Nehru has steadily denounced Pakistan as militarist and Western-orientated. He has been content in the argument over Kashmir smugly to rest on the fait accompli and has brushed off demands for a referendum or other compromise.

And now India's defence against Communist Chinese imperialism may come to depend on the goodwill of Ayub Khan's Pakistan. For it may become critical for India to free the half million seasoned Indian troops in Kashmir for the fight with China. Those

---

1   Shangri-La is a fictional place described in the 1933 novel *Lost Horizon* by British author James Hilton. Shangri-La has become synonymous with any earthly paradise, but often refers to Tibet.

116

half million troops would be of more value against the Chinese frontier offensive, than all the men he could possibly mobilise and train from India's 440 million people, even if he had time to train them.

Ayub Khan has now rebuffed suggestions from London and Washington for a kind of truce-of-God around Kashmir to allow India to turn her full strength against the Chinese. Quite on the contrary, Pakistan is vigorously protesting the emergency airlifts of American and British military equipment to India, and about the aircraft, which Mr Nehru hopes to get from Washington, along with MIG 21 supersonic jet fighters from Moscow.

No doubt Prime Minister Nehru could give a clear public answer to the morass of conflicting principles, which surround his foreign policy. He could say that India is doing the best it can in self-defence against Communist Chinese aggression. But I would be surprised if his private thinking were not much less clear and confident.

I would myself add that the survival of a democratic India in this struggle is as important to the free world, including Australia, as the survival of a democratic Germany in the heart of Europe. The stirring new life of India has given a leadership for freedom and human welfare in Asia. But, by the same token, Indian leadership in the principles of a peaceful international settlement has been a very mixed bag both for India and the world. When (as we all pray) she comes through this crisis, she will need to find some better substitute for the Nehru-Menon mixture of self-righteous hectoring of others, with expedient self-indulgence of their own interests.

Barwick's Proposals for Regulation of Monopolies

Monday 10 December 1962, Notes on the News

It is, of course, wise and correct for Commonwealth Attorney-General Barwick to make known, for advance public discussion, his proposals for statutory control of monopolistic practices. In 1959 he gave himself a lot of trouble over the Crimes Bill by being overseas during the early public discussion. But fortunately, this time, he should be back in Australia before the criticisms have piled up too much.

And there are bound to be plenty. One of the difficulties of this kind of legislation everywhere, is that the private and public interests involved are so strong and complicated that by the time everybody has had a nibble at the plan, its clarity of purpose goes, and it gets to look rather like a Chinese puzzle.

Sir Garfield did make it sound very clear when he said that the bill was aimed not at the bigness of businesses as such but only at activities, which harm 'free enterprise'.

Many books have been written telling us what free enterprise is, and many more will be needed before the lawyer and lay judges of the proposed Restrictive Practices Court, sitting in divisions all over Australia, could get much guidance from this particular phrase.

Most American businessmen said it was the end of 'free enterprise' when Roosevelt introduced his New Deal economic measures; but they still think that 'free enterprise' is a living ideal worth fighting for now in the 1960s, 30 years later. For that matter I remember that a century ago (though I wasn't there) many English businessmen thought that the end of free enterprise had come when the first really effective Factory Acts were passed to deal with safety and health conditions in British factories.

In fact, I doubt whether the new Act will finally use the idea of 'free enterprise' in its operative provisions. This does not mean that Sir Garfield was deceiving us; it only means that free enterprise is a notion too vague for courts to work with in imposing civil and criminal penalties.

The bill will surely use more precise notions, such as arrangements between two or more firms to fix prices or the terms of dealing, or to restrict output, restrict outlets, or to boycott or restrict entry to trade associations. It will cover also certain practices even done by a single trader, notably resale price maintenance, and the use of merger and takeover techniques to produce the same result as restrictive practices.

Sir Garfield proposes to outlaw with particular security, price-cutting below cost intended to ruin a competitor; collusive bidding and tendering by which many public authorities have been held to ransom in recent years; and monopolising, that is when a trader uses his strong position with regard to particular goods and services, to restrict other traders from entering the field or to make consumers pay through the nose. I wonder what this would do to the price of fish in Sydney, if it worked?

Apart from these last three especially naughty practices, all the others I have mentioned will only be unlawful if either of two things happens.

First, a trader who indulges in such a practice without registering a full description of it with the Registrar of Restrictive Practices will be acting unlawfully whether or not it is detrimental to the public.

Once he has so registered, he can carry on 'business as usual' unless the second thing happens. This is that the restrictive practice which he has registered has been brought before the Restrictive Practices Court, and the Court has found that it substantially reduces competition, and also that it works to the detriment of the public, for instance by exploiting the public or injuring or hampering the economy.

The three chief models of this kind of law in modern times are the American, the West German and the British. The proposed Australian act follows the British model, but I am glad to see that in a number of respects it has firmed up the weaknesses of the British model, particularly as to mergers and monopolies. It needed to, since there is the greatest doubt whether the United Kingdom Act, now six years old, has really made much difference to the effects of restrictive practices on the British economy.

The main contrasts between the British and American models are three. First, under the American Sherman Anti-Trust Law, there is no requirement nor even any facility for advance registration. Trades can carry on merrily until the prosecuting authorities catch up with them.

Second, under the American law, the guiding rules given to the enforcing courts are very much vaguer.

Third, the British legislation directs the court to determine the overall question whether the restrictive practice is detrimental to the public. No doubt that is a hard enough question in itself. But in many American cases, owing to the vagueness of the law, the court is often not very clear on what it is supposed to be deciding at all.

But then there have already been three score years and ten of pressures and pulls on the American system. We have yet to see what shape Sir Garfield's bill will have when lawyers and businessmen have really had their teeth into it for a while.

Yesterday, as a part of Human Rights Week celebrations, a movement known as Amnesty International held unusual programs in several countries in Europe, to keep the conscience of the world alive to the fate of something like a million persons who are imprisoned in 45 countries of our so-called civilised world, on grounds solely of their political opinions, religion or race. This quietly working but determined group, supported in England by such figures as Salvador de Madariaga and Ritchie Calder, sent observers in 1962 to no less than 11 countries, and has also drawn up a model Code of Conduct towards Prisoners of Conscience well worth the attention of the governments and peoples of the world.

Much strength to their elbows.

James Meredith and US Civil Rights

Wednesday 9 January 1963, Notes on the News

In a short autobiography published last September in the Saturday *Evening Post*, James H. Meredith, hero of last year's struggle to break desegregation at the University of Mississippi at Oxford, Mississippi, took as his theme some words of Theodore Roosevelt, 'The credit belongs to the man who is actually in the arena, whose face is marred by dirt and sweat and blood … so that his place will never be with those cold and timid souls who know neither victory nor defeat.'

Today comes the news, which we must still hope will prove false, that 29-year-old Meredith had announced that he would not register for the next term at Oxford unless there was an easing of the harassment to which he is being subject, and which is making it difficult for him to study.

The tense days and nights are still in recent memory when a new miniature civil war threatened in Mississippi, at just about the centenary of the great and bloody Civil War which liberated the Negro slaves. Five hundred US Marshalls confronted aristocratic student and citizen mobs of Oxford, Mississippi, brought to hysteria and violence by agitation both local and from other parts of the seething South, and encouraged by transparent support from Governor Barnett and the state authorities in charge of law enforcement.

The federal government under the leadership of President Kennedy and his brother, Attorney-General Robert Kennedy, as well as the federal judiciary whose orders set the stage for the crisis, gave to the world an inspiring demonstration of the American resolve to accelerate the movement for full civic emancipation and equality. Only last week six federal judges signed an order which may lead to Governor Barnett's punishment for contempt. In his immediate objectives the President triumphed. Meredith was not only enrolled but proceeded to attend classes and use the cafeterias and amenities of the university like any other student.

Not quite like any other student however. For the most part he had to be accompanied in all his movements by a bodyguard of US marshals. And in the cafeteria, the table at which he sat was a shunned table; and with exceptions so rare as to make world news when it happened, the word thrown at him was never hello!

In these stirring events Meredith showed his courage and guts, in face both of lynch-happy mobs and of cold, venomous hatred. And his own story shows in my opinion, the integrity of his motives. He was out to get an education, not to cause trouble; but he was not prepared to give up the right to get an education merely because prejudice and race hatred threatened trouble. If his insistence on his equal rights to education came to symbolise the rights of all his people, this made him prouder to take his stand.

So for the first half year, or semester as Americans call it, he strove amid all the difficulties to master his courses in American political parties, theories and pressure groups, and French and English literature. The second semester begins later this month, and, as a new burst of hostile leaflets was scattered over the campus, no one can really blame James H. Meredith for wondering if the strain would allow him to make any progress in his studies at Oxford, Mississippi.

Not only Americans, including many in the South but all America's friends, will agree with the hope expressed by Attorney-General Kennedy, that Meredith will find it possible to remain the symbol that he is of the movement for human equality, dignity in the deep South.

The UK and the Common Market

Sunday 10 February 1963, Australia Looks at the World, 1.45 pm

Public discussion of the Common Market affair has tended to circle around the question whether the crisis and its causes are primarily economic, or political or military. And even de Gaulle's explanations at the French National Assembly Reception this week seem to have blamed in one breath Britain's continued nuclear weapons tie up with America, and in another Britain's involvement in American plans for a free trade area. And in case this is too clear, the French President has now dissociated himself from what he was reported to have said.

In fact, when we look at the history of this matter of Britain and Europe since World War II, and at the questions now facing Kennedy and his advisers, we shall see that all of these aspects have always been so mixed together that none can be said to be primary. It is no wonder that Secretary of State Rusk has foretold a period of pause in certain areas of Western policy, following the Common Market crisis. The President and his advisers certainly need a pause.

Washington was already pressing Britain to enter a European economic union in the 1940's, and Britain (despite some early gestures from Sir Winston Churchill) steadily resisted this pressure in the following years. Washington's pressure continued right into the present crisis, when we find her almost boxing the ears of naughty children like Australia, who seemed to make difficulties about Britain's entry. Britain on the other hand, only 18 months ago, did almost a full turnabout, abandoning her resistance, and pressing with almost indecent urgency to enter the Common Market.

If we are to understand policy issues now facing President Kennedy, we must first understand why Washington has so persistently urged Britain to get into Europe, and why Britain resisted so long and hard.

The American pressure had a fourfold drive. First, Washington wanted to spur European economic recovery and relieve the American taxpayer of the gigantic burden of economic aid to Europe. Second, Washington long feared unstable government and even communist seizure of power in France and Italy, and regarded the more solid Britain as a stabiliser. Third, she wished to reassure France that Britain would be at her side in case of a revival of Germany, so as to obtain French cooperation in the build-up of West European defences against possible Soviet attack. Fourth, and surviving from another age and world, this policy fitted well with the hopes of many Americans even today for their country to return to the isolationism of its early history.

Why then did Britain resist both American pressure and Europe's beckoning? Basically I think because it is hard to change a view of your destiny based on centuries of successful experience. Whether in economic or strategic terms, Britain's outlook, at least since the first Elizabeth, has been across the oceans. After 1945 she was still looking mainly eastward along Mediterranean sea lanes, and the air lanes to the Persian Gulf, the Indian Ocean, Malaya, Singapore and Australia and New Zealand.

When not looking east, she looked west, still across the ocean, to Canada, the West Indies, Latin America, and the United States. And she came, for many good reasons, to look increasingly to the United States. First, for relief of her economic distress; second, because, being no longer herself mistress of the seas, American navy power was essential to her oceanic security; third, because America headed the select nuclear club of which Britain was a member, and last, because the idea of an Atlantic Union of free peoples, centred on what de Gaulle called the Anglo-Saxons, was dear to many British and American hearts.

When Britain finally decided, 18 months ago, to enter the Common Market, these reasons were mostly overridden. That does not mean that de Gaulle was right in questioning either her sincerity or readiness. For Britain may now have had good reasons for abandoning her old reasons. One good reason certainly was that the Common Market Six seemed to prosper so greatly and so quickly that membership came to outweigh almost all other considerations.

The adamant 'Common Market No' that de Gaulle gave to Britain, and the military No's! that he gave to Washington, re-open most of Washington's old policy stances which I have described, as well as posing quite new issues – let me mention but a dozen of these questions that the President will be struggling with:

1. Is there any hope still of preventing the Common Market Six from becoming an exclusive economic club whose operation will jeopardise rather than secure the economics of the free world?
2. Can the resentments against de Gaulle among the smaller members of the Six be used to check these exclusive tendencies? Should Washington try to split the Common Market Six further, and how?
3. If there is no hope here, ought Washington, at long last, to begin responding to the British wish for special ties, especially economic, with the United Sates? She might consider, for example, association with EFTA – the British-sponsored Free Trade Seven rival to the Six – and with other Commonwealth nations including Australia, in order to build both bigger markets and more strength for bargaining with the Six.
4. Do de Gaulle's positions on the Common Market, on the independent French nuclear deterrent, and his opposition to a NATO joint nuclear force, mean that NATO must be remodelled or cut down to size as no longer the main Western defence instrument? And,
5. Linked with this last – is de Gaulle shrewd or only silly in believing that the Soviet military threat in Europe is so small that Paris and Bonn can go it alone?
6. Is West Germany's complicity with de Gaulle complete? Or can Washington rely on Vice-Chancellor Erhard's declared solidarity with the United States, even as against Adenauer, he being Adenauer's probable successor? Where does Adenauer's recent

double talk about West Germany still looking to NATO, but wanting its own say about the use of nuclear weapons, leave him?

7. If de Gaulle's big power militarism proves to be only silly how does Adenauer's complicity with him affect Washington's pledges about the defence of West Berlin and West Germany generally?

8. Will Moscow try to exploit these Western disunities and uncertainties, and if so how, and how hard?

9. How does all this affect the promise of more fruitful negotiations between Washington and Moscow after the Cuban Affair, and the Moscow-Peking rift?

10. On the other hand, should not Moscow and Washington take some kind of common attitude towards de Gaulle brandishing H-bombs in his rather impulsive hand?

11. Underlying all this are two domestic questions for the American President. His record deficit budget this year demands a great revival of American business if he is to avoid serious trouble in later years. Is a freer-trade, lower-tariff association with British countries and with the Seven a safe way to his hoped-for revival of American business? Or,

12. On the contrary, will the President rather be faced by irresistible pressure from lobbyists, and the never tiring isolationists, for a revival of economic nationalism and protection of local US industries?

We must hope that Kennedy can persist in his policy for freer international trade which would assure a steady growth of trade between the United States and British and Scandinavian countries, and make in the long run for a sensible bargain with the Six.

We may feel that it is very confusing to have so many different questions all stemming from the Common Market-NATO crisis. If so, we should not worry. What is important is precisely to see how many and how different they are; and we can be sure that even Washington must find them confusing too. And for that matter these confused complexities are much more comforting and even interesting than the devastating simplicities of nuclear threat and counter-threat of recent years.

Mutual Espionage – Strange Case of Great Power Co-operation; Australia Approves US Base at North West Cape

Thursday 21 March 1963, Notes on the News, 1.15pm

It will startle some of you no doubt to hear that Washington and Moscow may be slipping quietly, and with mutual satisfaction, into a relation of friendly and informal mutual espionage. There has certainly been much recent evidence that this may be so.

The last incident took place about 48 hours ago, when high speed Soviet reconnaissance aircraft deliberately flew over a United States aircraft carrier on the high seas. They did this so openly that they were joined by American aircraft, which (as it were) escorted them until their mission was finished.

We also know from a Washington announcement that the United States has made no protest about this, that Soviet aircraft have done this kind of thing before and that US aircraft frequently make similar inspection of Soviet war vessels without Soviet protest. No doubt Moscow would say, like Washington, that no protest is called for because both the ships and the spying aircraft are on or over the high seas, which are legally open to all nations. But, of course, these governments have been known to protest violently about other things than breaches of international law.

Last Saturday Washington did formally protest against penetration by two Soviet planes, flying three to seven miles high at more than 400 mph, 30 miles into south-west Alaskan territory. They were apparently testing the sensitiveness of the US radar early warning system. Clearly this was as much a violation of international law as when the American U2 spy plane flew over Soviet territory a couple of years ago.

What is significant about the US protest is that it voiced none of the wrath and fire that Khrushchev used about the U2, but was mild and matter of fact. Indeed, according to US Congressmen, this was only one of a number of Soviet over-flights of American territory, relating to which the US protests have been not only calm but virtually secret. And the State Department has stated that Saturday's public protest would not be followed by other diplomatic moves.

But the evidence for a mutual Moscow-Washington indulgence is even stronger. For instance, before, during and since the Cuban crisis, US aircraft have been making regular flights over Cuban territory, to check the disposition of Soviet equipment and personnel. The mildness of Soviet reaction to this regular espionage matched Washington's mildness towards the Soviet trespasses just mentioned. During that period indeed, the US apologised for a US flight over Russia itself, and Moscow in turn made little of it.

What motives can Moscow and Washington have for tolerating what amounts to espionage of one against the other? Is not the spy the deepest and most dangerous enemy of the state against whom he spies? Is not espionage traditionally the most divisive activity between nations? How then can Moscow and Washington each permit the other to spy on it in this way? What common interest can they have in this? If they cannot agree to a system of international inspection either for tests for disarmament or against surprise attack, what sense does it make for them to allow reciprocal espionage?

Let me give you a short answer, which some other time I might develop more fully. In fact, when you strip away the verbiage, an international inspection system, if we could achieve it, would amount to a system of reciprocal espionage on terms agreed in advance by the parties. Each side has an interest in certain kinds of preparations not being secretly made by either of them, particularly those for a surprise attack. Each also has a common interest in neither of them knowing too much about other kinds of preparations the other is making, notably those for retaliation against surprise attack. If Moscow knows too much about American retaliatory dispositions, it might be tempted to try to neutralise them, and therefore risk a surprise attack; and vice versa. And both sides would suffer.

Now international inspection to warn of preparation for surprise attack seems unattainable, since at least one side does not trust any fixed formula to cover unforeseen future situations. And it is precisely here where mutual tolerance of more old-fashioned espionage, but in a new aerial form, comes into the picture. Unilateral aerial espionage can provide information that each side needs to warn it against impending surprise attack. At the same time, each side can shoot the spy planes down, at any point when it feels that they are getting or seeking the kind of information, which facilitates surprise attack.

The ditherings of the special Labor Party conference on defence concerning its attitude to the proposed US communications base at North-West Cape are now over, with an endorsement of Mr Calwell's policy of approving of the plan subject to conditions, which I believe, will present no insuperable problems to Canberra or Washington. It would have been tragic if the decision had gone the other way. The Labor Party has, I believe, enough sense of history and leadership to recognise that the proposed communication centre for the Indian Ocean area is as vital for Australian survival as was Washington's response to Curtin's historic call for US aid in 1942.

No doubt other world factors besides Australian security have led Washington to decide that her mobile striking power, including Polaris missile power, must extend to the Indian Ocean area. But the net result is to extend major American power beyond the island defence chain, which hitherto ended at Manila, into an area that is a vital bulwark to Australian security. We have as much to gain and as little to lose from this extension, as we had from the concentration of American forces and equipment in the south-west Pacific in the last war.

It would be childish of us, as it has already proved to be of a number of folk in Great Britain, to think that by unilaterally disarming or failing to arm, you can reduce the risks of living in our inescapably dangerous world.

The Suspension of Drivers' Licences – Legal Rules and Precedents

Thursday 21 February 1963, Notes on the News, 1.15pm 2BL

A lot of different questions, some very important, are involved in the many-sided row stirred up by the claim of the Commissioner of Road Transport to suspend the licences of drivers with bad court records, where a court has not seen fit to do so.

And many different elements in the community are also deeply concerned including, besides the government, the magistrates who try most motoring offences and on whose behalf the President of their Institute, Mr Stoneham, yesterday indignantly denied charges of magisterial laxness, and protested against any external pressures. All drivers are concerned; for them suspension of licence may even prevent them earning their living. Also involved are members of the public generally, who may be maimed or killed by drunken or reckless driving, and of course lawyers.

The special interest of lawyers is twofold, first because wild statements were made in parliament yesterday that lawyers were instigating magistrates to shirk their duty to impose adequate sentences, and that good lawyers were able nine times out of ten to get those charged with serious offences off with trivial penalties. Second, lawyers have a special interest – and even duty – to warn the community of interference with the course of justice, whether coming from bureaucrats, political ministers or anyone else.

Some questions that may be in peoples' minds can be disposed of very quickly. There seems no question that, as a matter of technical law, the Commissioner of Road Transport has legal power to add to a convicted motorist's punishment by suspending his licence, and that this power has been used from time to time.

The power was created in 1958 as one measure (approved incidentally by the NRMA) to reduce injuries and death on the road. After recurrent driving offences, a motorist is warned by the Commissioner that his licence may be suspended if he offends again. If he does offend again, his licence is suspended or cancelled unless he shows cause why it should not be. While there is an appeal against this to a court, Opposition Leader Askin claimed this was slow and expensive.

The Commissioner's powers complained of are therefore technically lawful. Yet, even apart from political intervention by his minister, Mr Walsh's powers have been the subject of protest not only by some magistrates but also by the New South Wales Bar Association.

These protests draw attention to the vital point that action that is technically lawful may still be a gross violation of the broad ethical and political ideals known as 'the rule of law', which in British tradition binds Parliament and the Executive as well as citizens. For judicial power to be exercised by a political minister without proper procedures violates this accepted ideal. For a minister to instruct an official to decide a matter, to which the official should bring an unbiased judicial mind is even worse. For an official to use even his legal powers, as Mr Enticknap seemed to claim the Commissioner should, to bring pressure on magistrates to stiffen up their sentencing, would be a graver violation still. And, further, to try a convicted offender again for the same offence would violate the distinct and precious principle of our tradition against double jeopardy and double punishment.

If, as Minister of Transport McMahon claims, his suspension of a licence is not an additional punishment for the last offence but is imposed in respect of the motorist's whole record, it might not violate the double jeopardy rule. But it would still be objectionable as giving what is essentially penal judicial power to a mere civil servant.

Moreover, the way in which the power has recently been exercised debars the government from claiming that the suspending power is not punitive at all but is only a safety measure to keep hopelessly dangerous drivers off the road. Last month Magistrate Hunt at Redfern allowed an appeal against a mere 12-day suspension, pointing out that a driver dangerous today could scarcely become safe merely by lapse of 12 days.

Our traditional ideals of the rule of law also demand independence for judicial personnel. If Mr Enticknap said anything at all like what was reported, he was very careless about this independence. It is true that our magistrates are not Supreme Court justices, but the mantle of judicial independence and immunity from outside pressure covers them also.

A conscientious Minister of Transport must of course strive for safety on the road. But, even if lenient sentences for serious offences were a factor in safety, the correct procedure would be for parliament to amend the law that judges have to apply, for instance by fixing more stringent mandatory penalties for particular offences or persistent offenders.

Opposition Leader Askin also suggested in the Legislative Council yesterday that parliament could establish an independent tribunal, before which the Commissioner could bring cases where he thought a licence should be suspended when the magistrate had failed to suspend it. Even this would be rather alien to our penal traditions; I am inclined to say that driving offences, like pure food and drug offences and many other statutory welfare and safety offences of today, are rather different from the classical crimes and that there must be a certain amount of flexibility in making them effective for the purposes we all approve.

Almost as important as the independence of the judiciary is the issue raised by charges that lawyers representing defendants before magistrates' courts unduly influence the magistrates towards leniency for their clients. This kind of charge shows a gross and dangerous ignorance of the basis of the rule of law in British countries.

The administration of justice in this tradition is based on the adversary procedure, in which each side and its counsel has the right, and counsel has indeed the duty, to present their case in the strongest and most favourable light that the facts and the law may warrant.

This right and duty reflect basic rights of all citizens, and interference with them is a threat to all citizens. And, as Bar Association President Meares pointed out yesterday, it is by each side putting its case well that the judge can best assess both sides of the facts and submissions.

There may be cases, indeed, in which this works unfairly against a party who cannot afford as able a counsel as the other side has. But, as between the government of NSW and a private citizen charged with a traffic offence, it is preposterous to suggest that the private citizen has some unconscionable advantage. The only conceivable basis for such a suggestion would be to say that either most police prosecutors or most magistrates were unworthy or incapable of the duties they perform. And it is this kind of innuendo, which explains much of the heat of these recent events.

The Hotline Moves Towards Implementation; West German Scientists Help Egypt Arm Against Israel

Monday 8 April 1963, Notes on the News, 1.15pm 2BL

The most constructive news that has yet come from the 17-nation disarmament conference (of nuclear and neutral powers) at Geneva came this weekend. Soviet delegate Tsarapkin announced Moscow's willingness immediately to negotiate details on an American proposal for a direct telecommunication link between the Kremlin and the White House, without waiting for a disarmament agreement; a Kennedy-Khrushchev or K-K Hotline it is already being called.

This proposal has not been much in the news before, but it is one that I have long thought would be a sensible and feasible one, better than crying for pie-in-the-sky ideas, like world government, or immediate complete and universal disarmament.

In April 1959 I put precisely this proposal before a special Conference on International Conflict at Chicago, called under the auspices of the Carnegie Corporation, and Northwestern University, to which I was one of the 72 invited delegates. I also spoke of it in a Chicago television program reporting this conference.

What is of more interest for ABC listeners is that I developed this proposal as one of the principal suggestions in the ABC Lectures for 1960, which I was honoured to deliver early in 1961. In August 1961, on the urgent request of a number of leading American foreign policy authorities, Harvard University Press published these lectures in America as a book under the title *Quest for Survival*.

In May 1961 advance page proofs of this book were sent by certain of these American authorities to members of the Kennedy administration. You will note that, according to today's cable, the proposal was first put forward diplomatically by the United States a year ago, that is, early in 1962.

When headway is so difficult on questions of war and peace, I make no apology for stressing that the ABC has thus helped spread an idea which comes to something. But I am also recalling this part of my ABC Lectures because what I there said about it in 1961 is still a good comment on today's news. I said that my final proposal concerned '... that short period, to be reckoned in minutes and probably not more than 30 of them, within which at some time, which may God forfend, either the Kremlin or the White House might have to decide whether to unleash the terrible deterrent or retaliatory power now held ready against what each regards as even greater evils. Such a decision would be tragic enough, even if the belief that it was necessary to take it were well-based. Yet a decision which has to be made in a matter of minutes may also be based on error of fact, misunderstanding of the adversary's intentions, or plain miscalculation of possibilities.

Both sides should at least be able to agree on steps to eliminate all risk that a decision to loose these awful weapons on mankind might proceed from some last-minute error, misunderstanding or miscalculation. It would I think be an important next step to ensure that effective, direct and immediate personal communications between those who must make these decisions on both sides, should be possible throughout the agonising 30 minutes of which I spoke. It would be the part of wisdom now, before such terrible choices are faced, to set up machinery, internationally guaranteed, to secure this continuity of personal communication under all circumstances, and up to the final moment. We are entitled to hope that the world will never reach such a final moment. But the minutes before such a moment should at least be made and kept available, beyond the faintest shadow of doubt, for this most solemn and fateful summit conference of all.

The State of Israel includes about 400,000 survivors of the Nazi massacres, in which six million of their kinsfolk were done to death by methods of unspeakable and unforgettable cruelty. Most of the adult population of West Germany lived under and at least tolerated the terrible Nazi regime that committed these abominations.

One of the most moving aspects of our harsh era of international politics is the mutual helpfulness which has been the keynote of Israel-West German relations ever since West Germany, under Adenauer's leadership, made a sincere gesture by offering a degree of restitution for Nazi wrongs as part of the conditions of her own re-entry on the international stage.

Israel was unable to perform the miracle, which many idealists demanded of her, of forgiving the guilty and convicted mass-murderer Eichmann. But she has certainly achieved under Ben-Gurion's leadership the near-miracle of not identifying the whole German people with Nazi atrocities, and responding with cooperation and self-restraint to Germany's efforts at self-rehabilitation.

This makes all the more tragic the crisis that has arisen between Israel and West Germany concerning the activities of German scientists who are admitted on all hands to be developing offensive missiles with which President Nasser of Egypt has declared his intention to destroy Israel. It also explains the otherwise puzzling reluctance of the Israel government to bring the crisis into the open, despite strong pressure at home and despite the fact that it believes that these scientists are also working on atomic, bacteriological and chemical weapons, forbidden under international law.

The matter was only brought fully into the open by a remonstrance of the Israeli Parliament on 20 March. More recently, Chancellor Adenauer has himself intervened and the Bonn Cabinet has issued a condemnation of activities of German citizens in areas of tension, and indicated that it would study the legal problems of controlling the activities of these scientists.

But, of course, it is not as easy as passing a law, which would be very difficult to enforce. The more likely measure would be for the Bonn government to keep closer track of the movements of its scientists, and dissuade them individually and as a group, on moral grounds, and on the grounds of jeopardy of their own careers in West Germany, from working for this openly aggressive and murderous Egyptian design. That Bonn knows how to do this kind of thing is clear from its own claim that it has already induced Professor

Sänger, former head of the Stuttgart Jet Propulsion Institute, who had been in charge of Egyptian missile development, to give up this work and return to Germany.

Experts in Death – The West German-Israel Crisis

Sunday 14 April 1963, Australia Looks at the World

Of the two million inhabitants of the State of Israel, more than one-fifth, or 400,000, are survivors of families, which perished in the Nazi massacres of 1941–1945. More than six million of their fathers, mothers, sisters and brothers were done to death, often before their very eyes, by methods of unspeakable and unforgettable cruelty. Tens of thousands of the survivors themselves are still maimed in mind and body.

On the other hand, most of the adult population of West Germany lived under the terrible Nazi regime, which committed these abominations. Some Germans, no doubt, never believed that such things were going on. Some Germans, especially of the churches knew, and raised heroic protests at great personal cost. Most Germans however, though they must have known, remained passive and silent while the Nazi minority went about its evil work.

Easter Sunday, which this year coincides with the Jewish Feast of Liberation from their slavery in ancient Egypt, is a day for human reconciliation, not for recrimination. And I have mentioned these facts of history because my subject today is one of the miracles of reconciliation of our times, that between the State of Israel and West Germany.

One of the most moving aspects of our era has been the mutual helpfulness between these two states, ever since West Germany, led by Adenauer, made his people's sincere gesture of sorrow by offering to surviving Jews a degree of restitution for Nazi wrongs, for the sake of Germany's own self-respect.

A number of idealists demanded a year or two ago the impossible miracle that Israel should forgive and set free the guilty and unrepentant mass-murderer Eichmann. It is too little noticed that Israel has performed the more sensible miracle of not identifying the whole German people with Nazi atrocities, and of responding with cooperation and self-restraint to Germany's efforts at self-rehabilitation.

The highest and most unqualified praise of the Eichmann trial came from the official West German observer. Though there are still no formal diplomatic relations between West Germany and Israel, contacts are frequent and close. There is much trade between them, and a permanent Israel Purchasing Commission at Cologne, which deals also with matters other than trade.

I am saying, in short, that there have been, on both Israel and West German sides, factors deeply encouraging for humanity, factors that cannot be explained away cynically; moral and spiritual factors of grief, repentance, humility, and reconciliation.

All this illuminates otherwise puzzling aspects of the current Israel-West German crisis about high-level West German scientists (Bonn admits at least 11) and the hundreds of German technicians, who are now busy building for Egypt offensive land-to-land missiles openly designated by Egyptian President Nasser to destroy Israel, and those Jews who survived the German Nazi massacres. Israel claims to have evidence that these scientists are also working to provide Egypt with other offensive weapons, not only atomic, but bacteriological and chemical – which of course are forbidden by international law.

One puzzling feature of all this is the restraint of the Israel government since it learned of these scientists' activities last year. Until very recently, Jerusalem avoided open friction with Bonn, but tried by official but private contacts to induce Bonn to check the scientists' activities, resisting strong domestic clamour for publication of a White Paper on the matter. Last week, the head of the Israel Security Service resigned, probably (we can only guess) because of Prime Minister Ben-Gurion's refusal to take the gloves off in the argument with Bonn.

The matter came more fully into international view on 20 March when the Israel Knesset resolved that the German scientists' activities were a grave danger to Israel's existence, declared it to be Bonn's duty to take steps to end it, and called upon world opinion to help in stopping this activity.

Israel's Foreign Minister Mrs Golda Meir declared her conviction that the German government 'cannot remain indifferent to the fact that 18 years after the fall of the Hitlerite regime, which destroyed millions of Jews, we once again find members of that people responsible for acts designed to destroy the State of Israel', the home of the survivors of the earlier massacres.

The Israeli government was sharply criticised in the Knesset debate for its tenderness towards Bonn. 'You invite German experts in education to Israel' charged right-wing extremist Begin, 'and they send experts in death to Egypt'.

Yet, thus far, Ben-Gurion has kept to his principle of reconciliation, that Israel looks in her relations with Germany not to the past but to the future.

His early representations to Bonn about the scientists first reached only the civil service level, a level still not fully free of officials continuing from Nazi days. The early response by German press chief von Hase was evasive, denying that any Germans were working on atomic, biological or chemical weapons for Egypt, and denying that Bonn could do anything about it even if they were.

On the same date, perhaps by coincidence, the Bonn Foreign Office published notes to certain Arab states, denying that West Germany intended to establish formal diplomatic relations with Israel.

Only after a sharp Israel reaction did the Bonn Cabinet issue a statement condemning German citizens who develop weapons in 'areas of tension'. Chancellor Adenauer, on holiday in Italy, also called for the papers for the first time, and it was announced that legal problems of controlling German scientists abroad were being studied. The Chancellor was also rumoured to be preparing a personal message to Mr Ben-Gurion. He is due back in Bonn tomorrow.

The Chancellor must obviously be deeply concerned with the matter, on principle, and he is also aware of the condemnation, by most countries of the world, of any German participation in the threat of renewal of this type of frightfulness.

The practical question is, what can be done? Some of the scientists concerned may be Nazi-type racists; but most of them are probably in it for the fantastically high salaries offered by Nasser. It is not quite as simple as West Germany passing a law to forbid her scientists to engage in certain activities abroad, or even putting penalties on this. Principles of free movement are also involved, and practical difficulties of policing a ban.

The more real possibilities are for Bonn to make greater efforts to keep track of the movements of leading scientists, and dissuade them individually, and as a group, from working for this openly aggressive and murderous Egyptian design. Bonn is in a strong position to do this on moral grounds, and on those of West Germany's honour and self-respect, and because it is also in a position to influence the long-term job opportunities of scientists at home. That Bonn knows how to do this is clear from its own claim that it induced Professor Sänger, former head of the Stuttgart Jet Propulsion Institute, who had been in charge of Egyptian missile development, to give up this work and return to Germany.

For Bonn to assume responsibility of this kind is essential to vindicate the principles of reconciliation of which Adenauer and Ben-Gurion are joint architects. For Ben-Gurion and Israel and the peace of the world, the threat of long-distance massacre by Egypt must not be allowed to loom too close. For that would face Ben-Gurion with the same kind of decisions, if on a smaller scale, which faced President Kennedy in last year's crisis over Cuba.

Police and Human Rights – UN Conference in Canberra

Sunday 12 May 1963, Australia Looks at the World, 2BL

Resisting police arrest, wire-tapping, police interrogation of suspects and universal finger printing have all made the headlines recently. These and other whodunnit items have been daily fare at the UN seminar in Canberra on the role of police in the protection of human rights, where I was the official Observer for the International League for the Rights of Man. You may have wondered how all this tied in with the United Nations and international affairs.

There is both a short answer and a long one. You can find the short one in other items of our daily news, where we have been hearing about the retrospective punishments, house arrests, detentions without trial and other outrageous provisions of the South African government's latest sabotage bill; not to speak of the savage dogs and fire hoses, which Chief of Police 'Bull' Connor in Birmingham, Alabama, is zestfully using against negroes demonstrating for recognition of the human rights which the constitution gave them a century ago. So the short answer is that, in our day, gross violations of human rights have grave international repercussions, and are a matter of grave international concern.

The long answer is that ever since the old League of Nations after World War I, human dignity and the human rights of each man and woman, which go with this, have been a concern of international law and treaties. The human rights of the worker have inspired the International Labour Organisation from its foundation in 1919 to our own day. Care for human rights inspired many minorities and anti-slavery treaties of the League period, binding under international law, guaranteeing men and women freedom form oppression and enslavement, and with channels of complaint and redress for individuals or groups whose rights were violated.

The UN story is different. The UN Charter has some human rights provisions (like the Preamble and Articles 1 and 62) but they are rather too vague to bind states and have no teeth in them. They mainly authorise the Economic and Social Council to call conferences and make recommendations.

Things brightened up a bit in 1948, when the General Assembly adopted the Universal Declaration of Human Rights. The 30 articles of the Declaration spelled out some of the basic rights in the political, legal, family, religious, economic and educational fields. But even this Declaration was not legally binding on states, but only an ideal to inspire them. It set up no machinery to deal with violations. A binding Covenant was supposed to follow, but never has, though the Economic and Social Council has promoted, with only moderate success, draft treaties on particular matters.

Yet it is a fact that never before have so many government officers talked so seriously about human rights across frontiers and at international gatherings. Through its busy Division of Human Rights financed by the UN budget, the Economic and Social Council carries on an ambitious educational program among state officials, not only about generalities of human rights, but about their detailed implications for the various departments of government and of social life.

The present Canberra Seminar on Police and Human Rights follows earlier ones on criminal justice in Baguio (Philippines), Tokyo, and Wellington. It is the first to focus on police. There will be seminars in Warsaw later this year on the rights of the child. At Bogota (Colombia) and in Africa in 1963 and 1964 there will be further seminars in a series on the status of women in the family. In 1964, too, there will be meetings on freedom of information at Rome, following one in New Delhi in 1962; and a very timely seminar on human rights in developing countries is fixed for Kabul, in remote Afghanistan in May 1964.

Mention of developing countries brings me back to the present Canberra seminar. What good, if any, has the meeting done for the participant countries, for international cooperation, and for human rights?

In answering this we have to bear in mind how very different among themselves, are the 21 countries who make up the Economic Commission for Asia and the Far East. They divide and cross-divide three ways.

First some, like Cambodia, Vietnam, Iran, and Malaya are, as compared with Japan or Australia, still undeveloped. Second, most of them, like Australia, New Zealand, India, Singapore, and Hong Kong inherit the adversarial system of the English common law; while others like Cambodia, Japan, Vietnam, and Indonesia inherit the public investigator inquisitorial criminal system of continental Europe; while still others, like the Philippines, have features of both. Third, some of the participants are struggling with emergency conditions, for instance of organised gangsterism in Singapore and Malaya, or threat of invasion in India; while others like our own comparatively happy country have more normal conditions.

One great service of the seminar has been to make the police and prosecutors of each country more aware that on many matters there are recognised international standards of police conduct, a kind of code of police ethics, by which they may sometimes be judged. They are likely to remember this when they return to their jobs at home. I would guess that even those who did a little 'white-washing' for the seminar shop window will feel pressure to bring things at home nearer to international standards. And this goes for the more developed countries, too. For instance, some charges were aired about Australian police treatments of Aborigines, and sharply denied by our police chiefs. Whatever the rights and wrongs, however, any prudent police chief will be rather sensitive about such matters in the future. And I thought it rather a pity that the state of Queensland was not represented at a higher level than an able inspector of police.

Again, some Asian participants even urged the seminar to declare more precise international standards about police respect for human rights, to help them persuade their home government do better. The seminar was thus urged to declare clearly that the state should be liable in damages for police wrongs to citizens; and also that illegally obtained confessions should never be admitted in evidence.

Further, some countries produced useful ideas for dealing with problems, which were new to others. Thus India and Malaya told us about their strict procedures for preventing police extortion of confessions. Though of British origin, they have not been tried in Australia, for example. And Singapore expounded its elaborate and ingenious method of recording on tape the events of a riot emergency as handled by police, so as to allow the legality of police action to be effectively scrutinised by the judges when the emergency is over.

And of course you all read of the debates between lawyers and police chiefs, especially between our own judges and commissioners of police, about the desirability of tape recording of police interrogation of accused persons.

On the other hand, one of my main criticisms would be that such seminars would achieve more if there were a better balance between the officials whose duties are in question, and other more detached experts. Too much time was spent by police chiefs defending existing national practices, and too little on ways to improve them. The most creative sessions were provoked by two or three participants who were not officials, aided by observers from non-governmental voluntary bodies who, strictly, were not participants, and had only a limited right to join in. The fault for this lies with the nominating governments, not with the UN.

Weighing all in all, this kind of confrontation of national officials with international standards of protection of human rights remains a practical and valuable service. It is far short of having legally binding international standards with methods of pinpointing violations. But in a world where human rights are so fragile, we should welcome every serious effort to check the tyranny which ever threatens from the abuse of political authorities and legal discretions.

Indonesia Releases Major Batch of Political Prisoners

Monday 2 August 1971, News Commentary, 6.55pm

Tidings that Indonesia is proceeding to release 50,000 political prisoners of their so-called Category C, will rejoice all friends of Indonesia, and indeed all friends of free government. These prisoners have been in detention since the abortive left-wing coup d'état of September 1965, in which many of Indonesia's leading generals were savagely butchered.

The defeat of that coup brought President Suharto to power. It also brought to an end Peking's great influence in Djakarta under President Soekarno, and established the basis for the present friendly relations between Indonesia and the Australian and American governments. Any Westerner with a democratic conscience must have felt the sad irony that the largely arbitrary detention of tens of thousands of men and women accompanied the turn of Indonesia towards the Western democracies.

Of the estimated 200,000 people imprisoned in 1965, there was some kind of 'hard' evidence of involvement in communist organisations only against 10–20,000. Against the vast bulk of rest, there was not even this. They were rounded up and detained under the vague head of 'sympathisers'. It is clear, indeed, that many thousands were caught up merely on the say-so of informers paying off old grudges, or coveting their cows or ploughs or village hut.

When I headed an Amnesty International mission to Djakarta in July 1969, in an effort to secure release of these prisoners, their conditions were lamentable. The already pitiable ration per man per day for all needs had been cut from 50 rupiahs, or about 13 cents, to half that amount. Many prisoners were in widely scattered camps outside Java throughout the islands, where central control was difficult. Even when on Java, prisoners were rarely accessible to their families.

Indeed, the central government was in danger of becoming itself a prisoner of the whole situation. The indiscriminate round-up and detention meant that tens of thousands people untouched by communism before, might have become converted to communism in prison. Both in humanity, and for the economy, leading members of the government wished to release them. But they had become haunted by the spectre of a revived communist putsch.

During my mission, when I conferred with Foreign Minister Malik and Attorney-General Sugih Arto, I was assured of the proposed early release of Category C prisoners. This Category C alone was then estimated at between 50,000 and 100,000. Shortly afterwards, in October 1969, Attorney-General Sugih Arto promised to release 26,000; and 30,000 were reported released by the end of the year.

No doubt that step forward was helped by the then recent formal end of the state of war in central Java. And certainly the promise now to release what appears to be the whole balance of 50,000 Category C prisoners is a sign of new governmental confidence in political stability, based no doubt on the recent electoral triumph of the officially sponsored military-civil service (Golkar) alliance.

In my book, however, the redemption of 50,000 souls is a boon in its own right, on which our neighbour's leaders are to be congratulated. We may hope that the same liberal mood may soon bring the remaining 14,000 prisoners of Categories A and B to early trial or liberation.

Big Powers Agree on West Berlin

Wednesday 25 August 1971, News Commentary, 6.55pm

So there it is, the first Big Power Agreement on West Berlin since World War II – Soviet responsibility for free access by rail and road from West Germany to West Berlin, and limited visits by West Berliners to East Berlin, in return for a Soviet Consulate General in West Berlin, and a formal ban on major West German governmental, and especially parliamentary, activities in West Berlin.

Seen in historical context, this agreement is the latest phase in a 25-year-old argument about the Potsdam Agreement on the future of Germany. The four powers all claimed that under it, Germany should be united. But they wrangled for years in the Allied Control Council over the tiny sub-question, which Potsdam left open – namely, whose united Germany was it to be – the West's or the Soviet's?

The contemporary context of the new agreement is the drive of West Germany's Ostpolitik; it is well to remember that only three years ago, Moscow treated moves for improved trade between West Germany and Dubcek's Czechoslovakia as a pretext for the lamentable invasion of Czechoslovakia. The events leading to the present changed situation have included last year's West Germany non-aggression treaties with Moscow and Warsaw, by the latter of which West Germany confirmed the westward shift of the Polish frontier known as the Oder-Neisse line, and also West Germany's virtual abandonment of the so-called Hallstein doctrine penalising third states which recognise East Germany.

But ratification of the Soviet and Polish treaties, and indeed the whole dialogue whereby Willy Brandt and Foreign Minister Scheel seek rapprochement and trade with Central and Eastern Europe, had to mark time pending the present settlement of the Berlin question.

Even if none of the four powers backtrack and all sign the agreement in the next fortnight, West Germany and East Germany still have months of negotiation ahead on technical details. This direct role of the two Germanys, giving international standing as a negotiating party to East Germany, is part of what the West has conceded for the sake of settlement. We are that much nearer to the position when, even for the West, there are two Germanys in law as well as the fact.

Can we expect that the two Germanys and the two Berlins may even reunite with the blessings of all four powers? I doubt it. Opposed ideologies and the vested interests of German politicians forbid. And, even more important, such a reunion would defeat the main object of the exercise, from Moscow's point of view.

More than ever, with Peking's activism, Moscow now wants to avoid hostile confrontations on two fronts. An independent East Germany is part of her *cordon sanitaire* against non-communist Europe. A united Germany, unless she herself controlled it, would breach this cordon. But the West, for its part, would not tolerate a united Germany controlled by Moscow, and more than Moscow, would not tolerate one, which she did not control.

The new agreement, then, will reduce tensions between the two Germanys. We may even hope that it may open the path to a so-called European Security Conference, straddling the old Iron Curtain. But two Germanys, we can be sure, will still be with us all the way.

Analysis of West Berlin Agreement; the Neuroses of Demonstrators

Tuesday 31 August 1971, Notes on the News

The Soviet press signalled approval this weekend for the agreement on West Berlin, and called for a cross-curtain European Security Conference as the next step. Chancellor Willy Brandt praised the agreement yesterday as showing that he was not engaged, as his political critics claimed, in a sell-out of Berlin. The East German spokesman has pledged a 'constructive' approach towards it, and the State Secretaries of both Germanys have fixed their seventh meeting about access through the Berlin Wall, hopefully for next Monday.

> Sufficient unto the day is the good as well as the evil thereof. No one should underrate the value of thus defusing one of the world's potential flash points, in West Berlin.

The main lines of the agreement are already clear. The Soviet Union has given way on some chief points on which it has been adamant in the past. It has acknowledged West Germany's responsibility for West Berlin, including its representation overseas. It has accepted its own continuing responsibility, alongside the other three big powers, for free access by rail and autobahn from West Germany to the enclaved city of West Berlin – former capital of the German Reich, now surrounded by more than 100 miles of East German territory.

In the past, Moscow has tried to fob off its responsibility on to East Germany, whose statehood had been recognised by Moscow and the Soviet bloc, but not, of course, hitherto by the Western powers. The further recognition of East Germany implied in the current negotiations is an important Western concession.

Finally, West Berliners, along with West Germans generally, would be allowed a limited access through the famous (or infamous) Berlin Wall, to visit their relations in East Germany.

Thus, we may hope, will end a quarter century of big power occupation of Berlin, with its accompanying charades and rituals. In all that time, instead of the united Germany which all four powers claimed to favour after World War II, the West and the Soviet Union each fostered its own 'Germany' and, until recently, refused to recognise the other's. Both

Germanys made their way, East Germany feeling constantly threatened by the prosperous 'shop window' of democracy in West Berlin. The barbarous Berlin Wall, now flanked by memorial stones for tens of East Berliners who have died trying to escape to the west, still stands as the Soviet-East German shutter on that shop window.

A main quid pro quo for the Soviet concessions is the formal ban on West German authorities treating West Berlin as the capital of West Germany, especially by official functions there of the West Germany's Bundestag, or its President or Chancellor. But routine governmental and political party activities, committee meetings, and visits of members of parliament remain permitted.

All this new sweet reasonableness springs from two main sources – first, West Germany's wish to improve her relations, especially trade relations, with the eastern bloc – Willy Brandt's Ostpolitik; second, the growing Soviet anxiety (now intensified by Nixon's bid for rapprochement with Peking) about her eastern front against China, and her consequent wish to stabilise her western front with Europe. Rumania in particular, where a Peking Chinese delegation has just pledged support for that country's independence, drives this point home.

Sufficient unto the day, is the good as well as the evil thereof. No one should underrate the value of thus defusing one of the world's potential flash points, in West Berlin.

It is, I suppose, a mere coincidence (despite recent troubles up there) that it is a Brisbane psychiatrist who has just given the fourth Australian Medical Congress in Brisbane an intriguing theory about the psychology of demonstrators. Dr N.E. Parker said that a two-year survey in Queensland University had shown that nearly all the social reformers studied there were found to have had early histories of psychiatric disturbance. They had a 'common background of emotional unrest and psychological distress'. Such individuals, while busy demonstrating (he said), 'get by quite well' and do not need psychiatric treatment. As a psychiatrist, he inferred that psychological release by engaging in demonstrations was good for the individuals concerned. And he also added that 'it is often the crazy ones who change the world'.

The tendency of neurotics to be leaders in demonstrations, if it is so, certainly does not condemn demonstrators and their causes. It would be overly simple and wrong to dismiss all demands for reform as products of neurosis. Each cause, and the arguments for and against it, must be seen on its own merits. Greater danger, I think, arises rather from what sensation-mongering mass media sometimes do with such causes.

Good afternoon to you all.

Dutch Gestures to Indonesia, and Other Major Power Relations

Monday 6 September 1971, Australia Looks at the World

President Soeharto has just waved farewell to Queen Juliana and Prince Bernard. After a triumphal week of state occasions, the Dutch Queen spent the weekend relaxing on the island of Bali before her departure, while Prince Bernhard went touring in Sumatra. At yesterday's press conference, before their departure, Queen Juliana revelled in the affectionate nickname 'Grandma', by which she has become known to Indonesian students and young people.

No doubt the turnout of enthusiastic Indonesians with Dutch flags and other signs of welcome was helped along by official government inducements to festivity, as tends to happen in Asian countries. But even this aspect is still very revealing of the important role which Dutch patience and the generosity of Dutch economic aid has regained for her in Indonesia, as well as of the new flexibilities of Indonesian foreign policy.

During the present Dutch state visit, the Indonesian government firmly committed itself, this time through Foreign Minister Malik to the Dutch foreign minister, not only to release by the end of the year 50,000 out of the 70,000 communist political prisoners it still detains. It also agreed to allow to return home to Indonesia, presumably under amnesty for rehabilitation, the younger members of the group of 30,000 Ambonese rebels who, after failure of Ambonese struggle for independence, were given asylum in the Netherlands.

The fact that these pledges are given to the Netherlands, a country which figures in Indonesian history as the old colonial oppressor from which Indonesia liberated itself by arms a generation ago, confirms the sense of security felt by the Soeharto government, after the sweeping victory of its supporters in this year's elections.

The mobility of policy of other powers towards Indonesia, probably flowing from the same elections, is also manifest in new initiatives of the Soviet Union. Indeed, the present post-ping-pong phase of international relations is promoting a fluid – almost a running – phase of diplomacy.

Soviet relations with Indonesia for example, have been pretty much in the cooler since the suppression of the PKI[1] communist putsch in Indonesia in 1965, which also led to the

---

1   Communist Party of Indonesia

ousting of Soekarno. In fact, the new military regime in Indonesia traced the unsuccessful putsch to Peking rather than to Moscow, and it was with Peking that it severed relations.

But because the hundreds of thousands of prisoners rounded up and imprisoned by the Indonesian government were dubbed ' communists', Moscow for some years pressed for their release. The Soeharto government moved steadily back into close economic relations with the United States, the Netherlands, and Australia while Moscow, which had given Soekarno's Indonesia about $500 million of credits, had to re-negotiate rather poor terms for repayment.

This was in 1969–70. It is only now, influenced again no doubt by the massive recent electoral victory of the Soeharto/army-promoted Golkar Party at the recent elections, that Moscow's diplomacy in Indonesia is warming up again. This week the first post-1965 team of experts arrived in Indonesia to resume work on a fertiliser project. And Moscow invited the head of the Golkar Party, General Sukowati, to visit Moscow in the near future.

In a world in which governments are so often so inflexibly wrong, we should take comfort in such signs of running diplomacy, especially when it runs in such healthy directions.

Washington-Moscow Hotline Upgraded; Khrushchev Buried

Tuesday 13 September 1971, News Commentary

It has just been announced that arrangements surrounding the so-called 'hotline' between Moscow and Washington are to be made more reliable.

Since that dramatic channel of communication between Kremlin and White House opened on 1 September 1963, the arrangements for it have depended on an adapted use of existing underwater cables and landlines across the Atlantic and various European countries. A two-way teleprinter system was available day and night, running through Helsinki, Stockholm, Copenhagen and London. The terminal points were equipped to transmit and receive communications in Russian from Moscow to Washington, and in English the other way. A two-way radio-telegraphic channel was also available via Tangiers in case of breakdown.

What is now to be done is to build the hotline arrangements into the satellite system of worldwide radio communications.

The hotline is, of course, an invention – probably the most important one for avoidance of war since the end of World War II – to deal with military emergencies of ultimate gravity. It is directed to that short period, to be reckoned in minutes, within which at some time (though we hope it will never arrive) when the Kremlin or White House might have to decide whether to unleash the terrible deterrent or retaliatory power now held ready against what each regards as even greater evils. Such a decision would be tragic enough even if the belief that it was necessary to take it were well based. Yet a decision, which has to be made in a matter of minutes, may also be based on error of fact, misunderstanding of the adversary's intentions, or plain miscalculation of possibilities.

Significantly enough, the initiation of the hotline took place in the aftermath of the Cuban missile crisis of October–November 1962, which is the nearest that Moscow and Washington have come to a nuclear confrontation. In our rapidly changing world we tend to forget how grave that confrontation was – and even more – what an enormous debt is owed to the late John F. Kennedy, and to Nikita Khrushchev, for the two boons which together they retrieved from what threatened to be a major human disaster. One was the Test Ban Treaty of October 1963, the other the hotline.

At this moment, when for the Soviet government Mr Khrushchev remains 'a non-person' even as he is lowered into the grave, the rest of us should give a kindly thought to that magnanimity with which, after his defeat in Cuba, this Soviet leader contributed to such constructive measures as the establishment of the hotline.

For by that device, to which both governments have since remained loyal, they reduced to a minimum the risk that either might decide to loose these awful weapons on mankind as a result of some last-minute error, misunderstanding or miscalculation. It ensures the continuity into those last-minute personal communication, for probing mutual intentions, between those who must make these decisions.

In historical fact, according to former President Johnson's memoirs of the period, the hotline was used more than once during the critical week of the Six-Day War in 1967, to reassure each capital that the other would not intervene.

The new satellite arrangements will make communication more fool-proof against mechanical breakdown or interference. And it is a fair guess that their political context is not so much Middle East or European problems, but rather that of the SALT strategic weapons talks, and the changing Moscow-Washington-Peking triangle.

Goodnight to you all, goodnight.

UN Considers US Proposal on China – How to Accommodate Both Taiwan and the PRC

Thursday 23 September 1971, News Commentary

The lobbies of the world's chancelleries are still buzzing with reports that only about 12 states, all but Japan smaller ones, are to sponsor the American formula on the China question. Under this proposal, the Peking government would represent China in both the Security Council and the General Assembly, while Taiwan would still remain a member of the United Nations, but without being represented on the Security Council.

At this morning's session of the General Assembly's Steering Committee, the United States sought to secure that the two parts of its resolution, one to seat Peking in the Security Council, the other also to continue Taiwan in the General Assembly, would be taken together when the matter is reached in mid-October. But this move failed, so that she will have to move back onto her second line of defence of Taiwan. This is to ensure that any move to expel Taiwan is treated as an important question requiring a two-thirds majority.

These tactics on the China question sometimes become hard to follow, and it is perhaps worth a minute or two on some technical points, which contribute to the confusion.

One is that under Article 23 of the Charter, a state called 'The Republic of China' was made a permanent member of the Security Council at a time when the whole of China was still governed by Chiang Kai-shek. Each council member is entitled to only one representative and each permanent member has a veto on any substantive action by the Council.

From the point of view of both Peking and Taiwan, the present argument is whether the Peking government of the People's Republic of China (which I shall here call Peking) represents the 'Republic of China' within Article 23, or whether Chiang Kai-shek's government of the Republic of China (which I shall here call Taiwan), represents the 'Republic of China' within Article 23.

Since only one 'Republic of China' and only one representative of it are eligible in the Security Council, it would make no sense for the US to support Peking's claims unless it is prepared for Peking now to displace Taiwan on the Security Council.

After Peking's defeat of Chiang Kai-shek and the latter's retreat to Taiwan in 1949, the Security Council, over Soviet objection, accepted the Taiwan delegate's credentials as representing the 'Republic of China'. And this was followed in the General Assembly.

But strictly it need not have been followed. The General Assembly could in theory also have admitted the People's Republic of China, that is Peking or mainland China, to General Assembly membership. There is no restriction on the number of 'Chinas' which can be General Assembly members, as there is for permanent membership of the Security Council.

It is the converse of this truth, one which is operative today, that the United States and its co-sponsors are now relying. They are proposing, in effect, that the Peking representative's credentials be accepted as representing the 'Republic of China' within the Security Council under Article 23. This would oust Taiwan automatically from the Security Council while still leaving it in the General Assembly.

The paradox is that the one point on which Peking and Taiwan agree is that the land called Taiwan is a part of the 'Republic of China', entitled to be represented on the Security Council under Article 23, though each of them claims to represent it to the exclusion of the other. And it is a consequential paradox that the main hope of saving the United Nations seat for Taiwan is to get her to disagree with Peking on the one point on which they are at present agreed. She has to assert, in brief, that the island called Taiwan is not a part of the 'Republic of China' within Article 23 at all. This may be one of the cases in which a rose by any other name might smell even sweeter.

The PRC – National Day, End of the Cult of Mao, Support Grows for Admission to UN

Friday 1 October 1971, Notes on the News

Today is the national day of the People's Republic of China; usually – but not this year – marked by a massive parade and a great banquet with long speeches. A Peking report says that the omission only shows how things are changing in China.

No similar comment has been made on reported moves away from the 'cult of personality' – in particular of the personality of 77-year-old Chairman Mao Tse-Tung. Poster pictures of Mao Tse-Tung are said to be disappearing from streets throughout China, and Peking Radio has been cutting out its regular quotations from Mao.

One explanation offered of all this is some kind of trouble over the succession to Chairman Mao – either because of Mao's state of health or that of his designated successor Lin Biao. Another explanation is that a military crisis may be building up on the Sino-Soviet border. And it appears to be true that, in early September, Soviet columns were engaged on mock offensive manoeuvres there, and that somewhat later Peking ordered a military alert, including confining border troops to their barracks.

Meanwhile, of course, other manoeuvres continue around the question of Peking's admission to the United Nations.

The pro-Peking bandwagon is still growing, and I think that some hard thinking should also begin about the political consequences, if and when Peking is admitted in the 1970s. Instead of assuming that Peking's entry will mark some new and glorious epoch, we should be asking some pertinent concrete questions.

It is only, for instance, in the last few years that Moscow and Washington have shown signs of learning to work together without vetoes, either in the UN or in SALT. Can we expect the UN to become a more effective and promising body by the entry of Peking as a veto-brandishing member of the Security Council?

At a time when the troublesome age of de colonisation is nearly over, and many new African and Asian states are plagued by internal divisions, will these states be helped or hindered by entry of a Peking which deliberately exploits these divisions as a means of competing for influence with the Soviet Union? It will be interesting to check a few years hence on the level of enthusiasm of the present Afro-Asian champions of Peking.

Let me add that, from the point of the United Nations' future, there was more sense in favouring Peking's seat in the Security Council during the Cold War in the 1950s, as I myself did, than in the 1970s. Washington and Moscow were then at loggerheads, and Moscow was still marking up its 100 odd vetoes. Peking and Moscow were not yet in conflict, and it is probable that Peking's vetoes would, at that time, only have rubber-stamped Soviet vetoes, and two vetoes are no worse than one.

But insofar as the hope now has grown for Soviet-American accommodation, Peking's admission means that, even when Washington and Moscow give a green light together, as hopefully they might (for example) on improving UN peace-keeping arrangements, Peking would almost certainly veto them.

It is right, of course, that mainland China's hundreds of millions should be represented in the UN; but we should not be too starry-eyed about the consequences. Peking's leaders have no monopoly of prudence and wisdom, as recent self-confessed excesses of the Great Leap Forward, the Red Guards and the cult of personality remind us. Nor have they any special edge on peace-loving motives, as their adventures in Tibet and Indonesia showed. Of course, other UN members are not paragons either, but we don't expect them to redeem the world.

And, of course, Washington and Moscow are not expecting this from Peking's admission. President Nixon wants to join a bandwagon which, in war-weary America, promises success at the next election. His moves towards Peking also give him useful leverage in negotiations with Moscow. Moscow itself is too embarrassed at this late stage to withdraw the support she pledged to Peking when their relations were in better shape.

A very good day to you all!

UN Replaces Taiwan with the PRC; US Compromise Rejected; Congress Reacts

Tuesday 2 November 1971, Notes on the News, 1.23pm 2FC

A body known as the 'Captive Nations Association', representing people in Australia whose native countries are now under communist bloc control, plans to demonstrate in Canberra next weekend against what is termed the expulsion of Taiwan from the United Nations last week.

This demonstration, as I understand it, is to highlight the threat to other small nations of the precedent set by the high-handed action of the General Assembly in not only admitting the Peking government but also ousting the government of Taiwan.

The Captive Nations spokesmen stress that the effect has been to exclude a nation of 14 million from UN representation. They point out that Australia, with 12 million people, and other small states with even fewer, might someday find themselves victims of a similar assault, by alliances among blocs of unfriendly Assembly votes. This echoes warnings from Secretary of State Rogers and Ambassador Bush last month (6 October and 27 October 1971).

The final vote against Taiwan on the Albanian resolution was 76 for, 35 against, with 17 abstentions. But this is very deceptive. A better test of the line-up in the General Assembly was the preceding vote on the American resolution, which would have called for a two-thirds majority for any resolution to expel Taiwan. This was 55–59, with 15 abstentions, which means that a switch of three negative votes or five abstaining votes would have saved the resolution, and probably with it a seat for Taiwan.

I have been talking as if the state of Taiwan was expelled, and the Captive Nations Association claims that this is a precedent for expulsion of other states. Actually, however, it isn't quite as simple as this; and the complexity is important enough for us to try to unravel it.

Under the UN Charter, Article 23, 'the Republic of China' is by name a member of the Security Council, and a state member of the Security Council is necessarily also a member of the General Assembly. That was the position before the recent vote, and it remains so after the recent vote.

All that the recent vote did was to change the representatives of the Republic of China from those sent by the Taiwan government to those sent by the Peking government.

This matter of representatives is a matter of credentials, and theoretically each UN organ, including the General Assembly, determines whose credentials are valid for its meetings.

You may recall, however, that before the recent votes the United States committed itself to accept the vote in the Assembly, on Peking's claims as binding for the Security Council also.

Admission and expulsion of a state from membership of the UN are legally quite different from rejection of credentials of particular representatives of it. Articles 4 and 6 of the Charter provide that admission and expulsion of members require a decision of the General Assembly on the recommendation of the Security Council. And the need for recommendation of the Security Council means that any of the permanent members, including now not only Peking China and the Soviet Union but also Britain, France and the United States, could each of them by its veto block any move to expel Australia or any other state from the United Nations. It is difficult to believe that one or other of the vetoes would not be exercised in the Security Council to block moves to bulldoze particular smaller states out of the United Nations. Even the United States, which for 20 years never cast a veto, has begun to cast them in recent years.

Two real points remain in the warnings about the effect of the Taiwan affair as a precedent for use against the security of other small nations. One is the danger that the so-called Great Powers may become so intent on their own games that they make deals among themselves, which then leave particular small powers stranded. Another is that the control of expulsion of states by the Security Council vote could be by-passed by setting up a puppet rival government of the victim state, and then approving that government's credentials. But, of course, setting up a puppet government is not an easy operation.

At a time when it is fashionable to rubbish everything American, the Senate's shock voting down of the annual aid program reminds us that Washington, from the Marshall Plan onwards, was the pioneer and prophet of a great program in worldwide human helpfulness, into which America has poured since World War II over $140 billion. By the same token, the wholesale cutting off of such aid in a tantrum over the excess of the Taiwan vote, is capricious and unworthy of that tradition. Today's statement by Senator Fulbright, and President Nixon's bid for a 'continuing resolution' to allow him to continue aid expenditure while Congress sorts itself out, indicates that the Senate's 'No' is certainly not the last word.

Good afternoon to you all!

US-Soviet Trade Expands; China Makes a Noisy Start in the UN

Wednesday 24 November 1971, News Commentary

Despite rumblings from the American right wing, moves for major Soviet-American trade expansion are to go ahead. Commerce Secretary Maurice Stans is on an 11-day visit to Moscow, welcomed by Prime Minister Kosygin himself, for what Mr Stans has called 'very thorough and serious' discussions. Proposed deals are like kites in the wind, tailed with hundreds of millions of dollars.

Why this sudden sweetness and light? Obviously, it has economic urgency at a time when the US economy is faltering, and Washington is engaged in monetary and trade poker games with Japan and Europe, about its drastic import surcharge. But the real point is that these American economic troubles give Moscow heavy political and economic leverage at the present time. And Moscow needs this leverage in the current context of Mr Nixon's impending visit to Peking, of Peking's admission to the United Nations, and of the 'big bang' for world revolution, with which (it has been well said) Peking made its General Assembly bow a few days ago.

Moscow, of course, could not avoid supporting the Albanian resolution for Peking's admission. But her sober feelings about Peking's progress must be very different from either the raucous glee of the other co-sponsors, which so upset Mr Nixon and the Senate, or the surge of hope that a new day was dawning, which affected most other delegations.

Even seasoned diplomats and journalists sought to prepare us for some new epoch. The Peking delegation, we were told, was going to make a low-key debut, and to become a sober constructive United Nations insider, instead of a raucous destructive outsider.

With all this rosy optimism, no one very much was asking whether Peking's presence would make actual questions that divide the United Nations easier or harder to solve. Everybody agreed that the great problems afflicting mankind could not be solved by a UN, which excluded a state with 600 to 800 million people. And it was rather taken for granted that China's presence would make them easier. Personally, I've always doubted this, though I shall be very glad to be proved wrong by events. I would doubt, indeed whether any problems would be easier, even if we supposed that Peking's basic objective was a far-sighted improvement of the human situation. Even before the Peking delegation's opening speech, China's past record, and the known facts about international politics, should have led us to realise that actually China's objectives must be different from this.

First, she must obviously want to use the General Assembly and her veto in the Security Council to deter any Soviet impulse to settle boundary and ideological disputes with Peking by a 'preventive' use of the Soviet's present superior military power.

Second, she must obviously want to use the UN as an arena for her struggle for influence in the so-called 'Third World'. The General Assembly's principle of one-state-one vote, for both giants and mini-states, creates an ideal forum for great powers who want to change the world at the expense of their rivals.

So we should not have expected Peking to present a temperate profile when she made her opening bow. And certainly she didn't. The Chinese delegates opened with a fiery call for the smaller members to join Peking's campaign against the Soviet-American-Japanese big power dragon. They presented this as an unselfish Chinese championing of the cause of the weak; but it is best understood rather as a stage setting for the new phase of the struggle for world power between Moscow, Peking and Washington, which opened with the invitation for Mr Nixon to visit Peking.

Thus seen, Peking's 'big bang' in the General Assembly matches the other, nuclear 'big bangs' which she has just made in the atmosphere. Why should Peking's assurances that she will never be the first to use nuclear weapons be any more reassuring than Washington's or Moscow's?

In these circumstances, Moscow's big business moves with Washington, like its bid for a European Security Conference and the related current contacts with NATO for a mutual reduction of forces in Europe, are aimed to quieten the Western front of the Soviet bloc, at a time when its eastern front towards Peking may become increasingly lively. For the Kremlin, risk of war on two fronts has always been a nightmare.

Pakistan-India Conflict; Bhutto Emerges as Pakistan Head of State

Wednesday 22 December 1971, News Commentary

The end of the military phase of the Indo-Pakistani conflict is now being followed by internal struggle in Pakistan, in which Foreign Minister Bhutto has emerged as the new head of state, and by diplomatic altercations on the legal and moral responsibility for the war, in particular of the issue of aggression by one side or the other.

> The new government of Mr Bhutto and the government of India will turn this tragedy into a triumph if they both demonstrate to the world that the principle of self-determination of peoples is valid not only against ex-imperialist western powers, but also among and between Asian peoples themselves.

In one sense, former President Yahya Kahn's proclamation on Saturday, 4 December 1971, of a state of war with India, amidst the confused military and air activity of 2–4 December, settled the latter question. For, according to the general legal view, that state is an aggressor, which first commits any of a certain list of acts, of which declaration of war is perhaps the least debatable. This test would point the finger at Pakistan.

This perhaps is too formal a test. To call a state an aggressor, as the Department of State at first dubbed India (and then retracted), is to talk about overall responsibility for the outbreak of war. And this must take account of the full context of both parties' actions, to determine which of them placed the other in a position where it had no real alternative to using force.

Some international lawyers argue that, under the Charter, only self-defence against armed attack can justify use of force. This is probably too stringent a reading of the Charter and it would also have absurd and immoral results. It would, for example, require a state, which knew that its enemy would launch a nuclear attack on it tomorrow, to wait until it had sustained this potentially fatal attack before using force to try and thwart it.

It would also compel a state, whose neighbour deliberately set about the mass genocide killing of its own population, in violation of morality and human rights, to stand passively by and watch this operation, and be called an aggressor if it tried to stop it.

When I invented this last hypothetical case in my book *Aggression and World Order*, in 1958, I did not expect it to arise so soon. But the case of India, Pakistan and the flight of nearly 10 million East Pakistani refugees into India in 1971, is even more striking than my invented case. Last March, when the success of the Awami League in the National Assembly elections led President Kahn to shelve the Assembly and arrest Sheikh Mujib, he also launched the campaign of military suppression of 71 million East Pakistanis.

India was compelled to watch mass killings variously estimated at 200,000 to one million people, across the border. To that wrong was added the resulting flight into India of nearly ten million refugees bringing with them dire threats of cholera and other epidemics, and enormous problems of food, shelter and medical care. After all international aid was in, the mere financial burden on India would have been over $600 million for the first 12 months and probably more thereafter.

India could scarcely have driven these unfortunates back into the terrors from which they were fleeing. Moreover, Pakistan denied that these wrongs were taking place and rejected any responsibility for her fleeing nationals. In these circumstances India was faced with a choice between inaction, leaving her crippled for an indefinite time by this disaster, or seeking to restore conditions in East Pakistan in which the people could return safely to their homes.

My own judgement therefore is that the substantial and moral as well as the formal responsibility for the recent war must rest on Pakistan. The new government of Mr Bhutto and the government of India will turn this tragedy into a triumph if they both demonstrate to the world that the principle of self-determination of peoples is valid not only against ex-imperialist Western powers, but also among and between Asian peoples themselves.

Australia Considers Recognition of Bangladesh; Sadat Hesitates to go to War with Israel

Thursday 30 December 1971, Notes on the News

Diplomatic approaches last weekend in New Delhi, Calcutta and Dacca asked for early Australian recognition of the People's Republic of Bangladesh. And yesterday a special Bangladesh mission arrived here to press this objective directly on Canberra. The mission will have to counter Pakistan's threat to sever diplomatic relations with countries which recognise Bangladesh.

The mission will argue that most of Australia's interests are connected with Bangladesh rather than West Pakistan, anyhow, and India will bring its own influence in support. And both will no doubt draw attention to the General Assembly Resolution 2625 of October 1970, whereby UN members were exhorted to support liberation movements, even against a sovereign state like Pakistan, if the government of the state concerned has failed to accord equal rights, self-determination and fair representation to all of its people. This, of course, is precisely where the government of Pakistan fell short when, after Sheikh Mujib's overwhelming electoral success in East Pakistan in March, it imprisoned him, shelved the National Assembly and sent in the military.

The recognition issue is also behind Pakistan President Bhutto's rather desperate current bid to snatch the brand of Pakistan unity from the embers of West Pakistan's military disaster. President Bhutto announced on Monday that he had begun a dialogue with the undisputed leader of Bangladesh liberation, who was last week elected President of the new state, Sheikh Mujib, within the framework of West and East Pakistan unity. After a second discussion, Mr Bhutto spoke rather vaguely of freeing Sheikh Mujib and warned other countries against what he called 'premature recognition' of Bangladesh.

All this is a drastic change from trying Sheikh Mujib for his life for treason, which had been going on for months before the war. He is being put forward as a national leader even in West Pakistan. But we cannot know the strength of it all until Sheikh Mujib is allowed to speak freely for himself.

On the refugee front, some of the relief officials who helped to estimate the number of fugitives from East Pakistan at nearly 10 million, are now suggesting that this figure may be exaggerated, and that (as was certainly the case with Arab refugees in the Middle East) many of those holding ration cards are not refugees at all, and that many hold multiple ration cards. In any case, only 200,000 have yet opted to return to Bangladesh.

There may, however, be other reasons than rations for this slow return, which is certainly bothering the Indian government and has led the Bangladesh government to assume responsibility for their return. The slowness probably also reflects continuing doubts among these unfortunates whether the rapings, killings, and general chaos they fled from are already under control there.

Retaliatory butchery too often follows in the aftermath of successful liberation. And the quicker the new government of Bangladesh ends such barbarism, the smoother will be its path to international recognition. And the Indian government, too, must recognise that continuation of arbitrary violence and murder are a serious block to its natural wish to repatriate most of the refugees.

Despite statements from recent top-level meetings with his Syrian and Libyan partners, and from the 18 member Arab League, President Sadat of Egypt appears to have thought better of his often repeated threats to resort to war against Israel in 1971. This week's special joint meeting of the Egyptian Parliament and Arab Socialist Union was probably called to endorse this better thought, and thus try to blunt any reaction against Sadat personally, for pulling back.

Since Sadat will not go to war, nor will Israel withdraw from all the occupied territories by midnight tomorrow, the final gist of Sadat's latest speech is that the conflict is returned for 1972 to the diplomatic level. Here, the chief bone of contention is the Egyptian claim that the basic Security Council resolution of 1967 requires Israel to agree, in advance of peace negotiations, to vacate all occupied territories.

In fact, that Resolution is ambiguous as to whether the withdrawal referred to is from some territories or from all the territories concerned. We know that this was a studied ambiguity at the time of adoption, aimed to get the parties together. Since the resolution also couples withdrawal closely with a reference to 'secure and recognised boundaries', Israel claims that the resolution should be the basis of a reconciliatory negotiation rather than a mere weapon of political warfare, which ignores her vital security interests and the lessons of her recent history.

Israelis as well as Egyptians will certainly breathe a sigh of gratitude as 1972 opens without violence. On Monday, Prime Minister Golda Meir said that President Sadat would prove himself 'a great man and a great leader' if he resisted the pressures to open fire. He has qualified for that compliment. And he will consolidate the claim to greatness if he uses 1972 to bring the matter to a negotiating table, at which neither side lays down preconditions and each side fully explores the limits of the other's positions.

Nixon Ends China Visit, an Analysis of Interests Common to the US and China

Monday 28 February 1972, Notes on the News

What the French paper *Le Figaro* called 'the trip of the century' has ended with Mr Nixon's hopeful comment about 'the week that changed the world', a slogan adapted oddly enough from a book about the Russian Bolshevik Revolution of 1917.

The wording of the communiqué was apparently wrangled about right until Premier Chou En-Lai waved goodbye to Mr Nixon, at Shanghai. And it contains very little to support most of the wild theories of the Peking meetings that have been circulating.

Among theories thus discredited are those of an emerging Peking-Washington alliance against Moscow, a sell-out of Taiwan by Washington, a sell-out of Hanoi by Peking, a new and beautiful friendship between the people of China waving Little Red Books and the people of America, each side led by its 'Big Brother'.

On these and most other serious issues, except perhaps the presence of about 9,000 US troops in Taiwan, the communiqué merely restates the well-known differences between the parties. And even as to those troops, the American statement of intention 'progressively' to withdraw them 'as the tensions in the area diminishes' is only of a token character. After all, the Nixon doctrine proclaimed this intention three years ago, and it is still conditional on the reduction of tension in the area, which of course also implies that Peking is not going to do anything rash.

The realities of the Peking meeting are to be seen, I believe, not in the rambling communiqué, but in certain objectives which both sides achieve from the mere fact that the meeting took place.

First of all, Messrs Nixon and Chou En-Lai both needed political diversions from serious political trouble at home. Nixon seeks a new image of world peacemaker and Chou En-Lai, after a decade and more of false starts and divisive power struggles since the Great Leap Forward, wants to be seen in China as an Asian and world leader, to whom, in the ancient Chinese style, other world leaders might delight to kow-tow.

Second, Messrs Nixon and Chou En-Lai both have parallel interests in using the fact of their meeting as a lever against Moscow. For Peking's leaders it may not be true that they hate Soviet communism more than US capitalism, but it certainly is true that they fear it more. They fear unrest on the Sino-Soviet-frontier, along which their infant nuclear arms industry lies mostly exposed. For Washington, the immediate threats are not from China, but for continental America from Soviet nuclear ICBMs and submarines, and on the oceans from the Soviet Mediterranean and Persian Gulf fleets. This shared fear amounts not to an axis, much less an alliance; but to each side seeking for its own particular purposes, more leverage against its antagonist.

Third, besides these symmetrical interests, the two sides have certain complementary interests. Peking China, though it has tested nuclear weapons, still has to acquire the massive industrial base necessary for it to become a first rank nuclear power. Admission to this club is far more important to her than admission to the United Nations.

Peking, therefore, is hungry for capital, skills and new materials on which the growth of major industrial power depends, at the very time when (after last year's economic and financial crisis) the United States is seeking major outlets for her vast industrial output and her growing technological underemployment.

Fourth and finally, both Peking and Washington are, in different ways, at a turning point in their relations with Japan. Major Japanese industrialists have long been seeking to get in on Chinese development. At the moment only two percent of Japanese imports go to Peking China, far less than goes to Taiwan. And hitherto, this has been a main reason for Tokyo's refusal to agree to Peking's preliminary demand that she renounce her 1952 peace treaty with Taiwan, which underpins Japanese-Taiwan relations.

In this respect, then, Mr Nixon's visit gives Peking additional leverage against Tokyo, as well as against Moscow; while for Washington it serves as another round in the running economic battle with Tokyo, which was central to Nixon's crisis monetary measures and 10 percent surcharge, which so rocked the world in the last months of 1971.

If all this places the motives of Messrs Nixon and Chou En-Lai on rather humble and earthly levels, we should still not underrate the importance of the possible effects. Not least of those is the expansion of great power politics in Asia from a bipolar frame dominated by Moscow and Washington, into a multipolar one in which Peking and Tokyo (and possibly India) are likely to be additional actors. This would make great power politics much more complex; but it may well also bring them onto a less aggressive, less dangerous and less costly level.

Good afternoon to you all.

Indira Gandhi Returned to Power in India; UK and China Establish Full Diplomatic Relations

Wednesday 15 March 1972, Notes on the News

The sweeping electoral victory of Prime Minister Indira Gandhi's New Congress Party this week is an event of major importance, not only to India, but to all the developing nations of the African and Asian worlds, and to the West.

Through all his trials and tribulations, Indira Gandhi's father, the great Jawaharlal Nehru, maintained one steady triumph. In a period when efforts at democratic government toppled like ninepins in Asia and Africa, he vindicated in action his faith in representative democracy for the second most populous nation, and one of the most impoverished nations, of Asia. And he maintained legal traditions, watched over by independent judges inherited from the British, and invented whatever machinery was necessary to make manhood suffrage work under Indian conditions.

There is no doubt about Mrs Gandhi's victory. After the week-long voting in the vast subcontinent, by a largely peasant and illiterate population, it is clear for the first time since a Congress Party led India into independent nationhood, that it will be in a position to rule effectively in all the 21 states as well as at the centre. The Opposition Congress, which split away two years ago, has lost the two major states of Gujarat and Mysore. Even in West Bengal, which many thought would be affected by separatist movements towards Bangladesh, Mrs Gandhi's party has swept in, in 126 out of 130 declared seats, leaving the Marxists-Socialists with only three or four seats.

The Congress Party split threatened throughout Nehru's later years. After so long in power, the Party became ridden with vested interests, corruption, lassitude and nepotism. Many politicians who had joined with Nehru in the struggle for independence became strange and uneasy bedfellows with a Prime Minister of basically socialist vision. Prime Minister Nehru would neither impose his vision nor abandon it; and right-wing leaders would not accept and could not destroy it. The Party dared not lose the charisma of a Nehru who wore also the mantle of Mahatma Gandhi. In the results many basic policies at home and abroad were blunted and confused, and frustrated.

In loyalty to the Mahatma's teaching, Nehru dreamed of taming great power rivalries by mediation, non-violence or moral preachment. I well remember watching him acknowledge in 1961 that India's long frontier with China had 'come alive'. He was in deepest sadness, but it was obvious that he had no response in action.

Before his death, he was to see the part of India nearest to the recent hostilities with Pakistan invaded by the forces of Peking. Having thus made his point about India's weakness, and apparently pricked the bubble of Nehru's image as a leader in Asia, Mao withdrew his forces.

Nehru's neutralism had kept India's relations with the Western world, and her economic aid, at a low level, further complicating his domestic problems, and reflecting on India's international stature. As a result, Peking's support of Pakistan in the chronic quarrel with India over Kashmir, when joined with Peking's simmering frontier claims, placed India's whole future under a cloud.

Why is it that, where Nehru failed, his daughter Indira Gandhi, whom no one (including herself) would regard as equally great, succeeded so brilliantly?

Partly, of course, it is a matter of changed circumstances. At home, for example, there has been the so-called 'Green Revolution' in agriculture, enabling India to aspire to feed herself; and abroad, there is the open rift between Moscow and Peking.

But the reason for the daughter's comparative success may also lie in Nehru's very greatness. His role, for example, as the historic Congress Party leader, barred him from splitting the party on issues like corruption and socialism. But Indira Gandhi could face such problems without the baggage of history.

The mystique of Nehru's relations with the Indian masses, as their guru as well as Prime Minister, also encouraged him to put off the need to act. He rested as it were on his mystique. But his daughter inherited only a little of this mystique, not enough to rest on. She dealt with the obsolete rajahships, as she dealt with the Congress Party right wing, in terms of practical political goals, which would win votes and keep her in power.

Nehru was committed by his bonds with the Mahatma to precepts of non-violence, neutralism, and rejection of power, even though on issues like Kashmir and Goa he sometimes made convenient exceptions. But Nehru's persistent vision of himself as a neutralist and mediator largely defeated his foreign policies.

Mrs Gandhi, on the other hand, faced up to the fact that the combined threats from Karachi and Peking had to be met by rapprochement with Moscow. While still talking neutralism from time to time, she had no illusion that you can drive away the realities of international politics by verbal incantations.

The folly of Pakistan's former military rulers in their cruel repression of the rights of the people of East Pakistan, driving nearly ten million of them into India, played into the hands of Indira Gandhi's new realism. The military victory, and the creation of a friendly neighbour – Bangladesh, so widely recognised already that even Canberra and Washington are now in line – has also proved decisive in domestic politics.

After the communist military victory in 1948, which drove the Nationalist government of China off the mainland on to Taiwan, the British Labour government hastened to recognise the People's Republic of China (in 1950), and proposed the exchange of ambassadors. Peking kept London standing on the doorstep for years before agreeing to any diplomatic exchanges and only now, 24 years later, has a British government succeeded in getting agreement to raise its representation in Peking from a chargé d'affaires to an ambassadorial level. The new exchange is tied, of course, to Britain's recognition of the People's Republic of China as the sole legal government of China, to acknowledgment that the People's Republic claims sovereignty as a province over Taiwan, and to its closing of the consulate that it has maintained on Taiwan for a hundred years. There is really nothing dramatic about this. It is in line with the position of Canada and a number of other states, which have noted Peking's claim to Taiwan, but stopped a tiny bit short of full acceptance of it.

North Vietnamese Attack Hue and Press for Resumption of Talks; Soviets Welcome Nixon; Whitlam Takes a Stand

Monday 24 April 1972, Notes on the News

The main North Vietnam tank force that attempted, 26 days ago, a blitzkrieg capture of strategic points Quảng Trịand Huế, in the northernmost Military Region 1 of South Vietnam, was frustrated by the South Vietnamese 3rd Division, with American air cover. Thereafter two North Vietnamese divisions thrust down from the Cambodian sanctuary in an enclosing movement on both sides of the central base of Military Regions 2 (the so-called highland region) at An Lộc, 60 miles north of Saigon on main Highway 13. In Military Region 3 another division and more, also from Cambodia, are threatening Saigon's communications to the north with An Lộc, and to the west across Highway 1. The South Vietnamese defenders of An Lộc have just repulsed still another four-pronged assault. Heavy fighting was reported yesterday 50 miles from Saigon, but a direct attack on Saigon, like that of the Tet Offensive of 1968, is not yet in view.

The response on the ground has come from the forces of South Vietnam, with some ambiguous role of American advisers and American tactical air support. The main American aid, however, has been by strategic air strikes both by B52 bombers, and naval carrier-based fighter-bombers. As of yesterday, the US had 59 ships in the area, including three aircraft carriers and three cruisers; three of its smaller ships have this week suffered damage from North Vietnamese MiG-21s. The main American air strikes have been against supply trails and fuel dumps, warehouses and other military supply depots ranging to the outskirts of Hanoi, as well as on ships and facilities in Haiphong where (as if symbolically) two Soviet cargo ships with supplies for Hanoi were hit. Moscow apparently contented itself with a sharp protest, which the US Ambassador in Moscow was summoned to receive.

Arrangements for President Nixon's visit to Moscow are nevertheless still going forward on a routine if cool level, down to details of side visits to Leningrad and Kiev. And this despite Mr Nixon's rather obvious warning in a speech given in Ottawa that 'great powers cannot avoid the responsibility for the use of arms by those to whom they give them.' The Moscow reaction is mild indeed, if we remember that, a few years back, the late Mr Khrushchev called off his summit talks with President Eisenhower over the U2 spy plane incident, at a moment's notice.

Why this mildness? Well, I think Moscow's reaction is mild because Moscow needs Nixon's visit rather more than Washington does, for reasons related to Peking. The Moscow visit is designed, after all, to reassure Moscow that Nixon and Chou En-Lai are not forging an axis against the Soviet Union. To call off the Moscow visit in a huff might well make such an axis more likely.

Another question is why the North Vietnamese and National Liberation Front delegations in Paris are pressing so hard for a resumption of the Paris talks, even while freely admitting their own initiative in resuming full-scale war with all its tragic horrors. The delegations this week were taking a curiously legalistic and technical line. This is that President Johnson's order to cut back the bombing of North Vietnam was unconditional. They are saying, in effect, that this 1968 order continues to bind Washington regardless of their own renewed large-scale invasion of South Vietnam.

Those who find such a demand fair and just, like the left-wing Labor group in Victoria, which has recorded its wish for the military success of North Vietnam's and NLF's new offensive, raise great problems for all who try to be objective and humane, especially for those of us who joined in the broad-based call for withdrawal of American forces.

The basis of that call was rejection of mere military solutions. It was surely not that North Vietnam should be allowed the special privilege of achieving military victory after being massively armed with 500 Soviet built tanks, missiles, and artillery. If that was what the leaders of the moratorium demonstrations meant, whether here or in other countries, then many thousands of people who were persuaded by them were sadly misled.

Caught in this poignant position by the Victorian left-wing pronouncement, the Leader of the Opposition, Gough Whitlam had the fine political courage to speak plainly last week. He declared that 'any view that there should be military victory for either side is not the policy of the Australian Labor Party, has not been the policy of the Australian Labor Party and never will be the policy of the Australian Labor Party'. I rather think that he spoke, not only for most members of the Labor Party, but for most other Australians as well.

It is one of the most dangerous ironies of our age that only the one-eyed partisan (and I do not mean Mr Whitlam) can consistently recommend simplistic solutions for its more complex problems. Such simplistic solutions are so far distant from the actual problems that they never have to suffer the ordeal of being put to the test. So the simplest claims can continue in unabated self-righteousness or partisanship regardless of the stubborn and changeful facts.

According to the latest cables, the leader of the North Vietnam Paris delegation, Madame Bin now explained her country's massive new initiative for military victory. She claims it is a reply to 'the American strategy of Vietnamisation'. Since Vietnamisation is only the other side of the withdrawal of American combatant land forces, this seems to say that unless South Vietnam is left militarily helpless when the Americans withdraw, North Vietnam will seize it by military victory. That, I grieve to say, does not seem like a path to political settlement.

Calwell and Chipp Clash Over Multiculturalism; The Politics of Immigration

Tuesday 9 May 1972, Notes on the News

One regular peril to wise government is that in the struggle for power, false issues replace real ones; when one contender for power thinks that he can win by taking a certain stand. Recent examples of this are Mr Wilson's stand on entry to the Common Market, President Pompidou's rather phoney plebiscite over British entry, and Christian Democrat leader Barzel's manoeuvres against ratification of the West German treaties with Warsaw and Moscow.

Needless to say we have this kind of thing in Australia too. When the Minster for Customs, Don Chipp, recently pressed his vision of Australia as a future 'multiracial society', veteran Labor leader Arthur Calwell violently denounced it. 'No red-blooded Australian', he declared, 'wants to see a chocolate coloured Australia'.

In the resulting altercation, Minister Chipp was supported not only by senior Australian diplomats and by his colleagues, but by Labor's Deputy Leader in the Senate. It almost looked like a bipartisan or non-partisan immigration policy, with only Mr Calwell, the architect of our mass immigration policy, shortly to retire from politics, opposing it.

But please notice what really happened. Mr Chipp's colleagues, in supporting him, highlighted that the government's objective was still what Dr McKay called a 'homogeneous' or rather 'united' Australian society. Mr Chipp, without renouncing multiracialism, explained that what he meant was really that the government aimed at an 'essentially homogeneous and gradually changing' society, avoiding the 'untold agony of racial strife'.

The question of non-European immigration thus rested somewhere between Mr Chipp's 'multiracial society', and Dr McKay's 'unity and homogeneity'. At this point, Prime Minister McMahon, from a press conference in Western Australia, pointed out that 9,000 non-European migrants had been admitted for settlement in each of the last three years. This disproved any government racialism. The government's criteria aimed to preserve the unity and homogeneity of our society, and avoid admission of individuals who could not be integrated into Australian society within a generation.

> Questions are now being raised about Australia's attitude in case political and military collapses in South Vietnam produce a flood of refugees seeking to escape from political reprisals by a victorious north. These are ... questions of plain humanity towards persons faced with death or degradation unless they are given a new home. Australia should join vigorously with other humane communities in relieving its share of this tragedy.

Then came the party-political point, that Labor's policy would lead to excessive intake of non-assimilable migrants, including not merely non-Europeans, but also southern Europeans. Labor Party policy (he said) hinged on sponsorship by friends and relatives, and it was southern Europeans, Middle Easterners and non-Europeans who were strong on sponsoring an ever-widening chain of their kinsfolk and friends.

Only a few years ago, when some of us launched the Immigration Reform Association Branch in New South Wales, the so-called White Australia policy still underlay the attitudes of both parties. On the face of it we should be gratified that, within a decade, Australian immigration policy has moved to openly stated criteria free of racial and religious discrimination.

The remaining differences between the parties appear to be two. The first is Labor's sponsorship criterion, which, Mr McMahon claims, would yield too many unassimilable south European and non-Europeans. The second, to which Mr McMahon similarly objects, is that Labor would extend assisted passages without discrimination also to non-Europeans.

All this is interesting. But how do these respective immigration policies look from the respective immigrants' point of view? Principle is fine, but what about population, about how many are to be admitted? If the total is to become nominal, then heated argument about principles of selection may win or lose votes at elections, but will make little difference to well-qualified people who want to start life anew in Australia. And, in particular, how should we put together immigration design and zero population growth, which is now becoming a popular political catchword?

A demographic inquiry about optimum population levels for Australia is only now going forward. Over that inquiry, and over the attitudes of both parties, and of all of us as electors, hangs the question to which no one has an answer.

Liberal minded people, who helped to purge racial elements from our immigration policies, are largely the same people who are now gravely concerned about ecology, population growth and the environment, and who clamour for zero population growth. Tenderness for the environment now overlies their tenderness towards less privileged people who wish to settle in Australia.

The realities of future immigration policy turn much more on which tenderness wins this conflict than on arguments about unity, homogeneity and multiracialism.

Questions are now being raised about Australia's attitude in case political and military collapses in South Vietnam produce a flood of refugees seeking to escape from political reprisals by a victorious north. These are different questions from any I have mentioned. They are questions of plain humanity towards persons faced with death or degradation unless they are given a new home. Australia should join vigorously with other humane communities in relieving its share of this tragedy.

Good afternoon to you all, good afternoon.

UK Considers Review of Laws of Evidence and Procedure; US Supreme Court Declares Death Penalty Unconstitutional

Tuesday 4 July 1972, Notes on the News

The pressure for criminal law reform in common law countries like the United Kingdom and Australia has been on dramatic issues like the death penalty, homosexual behaviour in private and abortion. Progress has varied from country to country, but on the whole the United Kingdom has maintained a degree of leadership.

In terms of drama, the current proposals by the English committee headed by Lord Justice Edmund Davies may not seem too sensational to laymen. The 14-man committee, of lawyers, law teachers and judges, has reported in favour of four main changes in criminal procedure and evidence, in which Attorney-General McCaw has already indicated a close interest for New South Wales.

The new proposals are important far beyond their dramatic interest. Most of us, of course, read more avidly about murders than about procedure and evidence. But we do so as spectators; very few of us expect to be charged with murder and the like, or to be directly concerned with the law.

Changes in criminal procedure and evidence, however, affect at one swoop, persons charged with any offence whatsoever, over an ever-widening range of offences affecting all classes in the community; for instance, traffic offences and new kinds of white collar crimes that are of concern to professional and business men under company and security exchange control and regulation.

The Davies Committee's proposed changes are reported to be:

First, it would abolish the rule requiring the police to warn an arrestee that he need say nothing, and that anything he does say may be used in evidence against him. It would also relax the related rules about his right to remain silent under interrogation.

Second, it would put more pressure on an accused to testify, and thus expose himself to cross-examination, by making his silence in court subject to comment by the prosecution. In other words, it would whittle down the present privilege against forced self-incrimination.

Third, it would compel wives and husbands to testify against the accused spouse, if called on, thus preferring efficient prosecution to mutual confidence in family relations.

Fourth, it would allow use of the accused's prior convictions as evidence of his guilt of the later offence. The present law forbids such use, in order to protect the accused against jurymen's temptation to leap to the conclusion that if a man has a bad record, he must be guilty of the present charge.

These changes would impair safeguards of liberty long treasured in British communities. The reason offered for making them is that the present rules hamper detection and prosecution, especially of organised crime. For instance, it is said, if an accused can remain silent, this gives his organisation ample time to fabricate an alibi for a trial months later, when the police have no hope of checking it. Lord Chancellor Hailsham spoke in the spirit of these proposals when he told magistrates in April last that excessive severity is better than excessive leniency, because the appeal court can reduce sentence but cannot raise it.

We should not be easily persuaded by such sweeping arguments. Each proposal has to be taken at its own merits. For instance, it may be that admitting the accused's prior convictions is sensible in cases involving similar crimes, especially as mostly now in England, indictable offences are tried not by juries, but by judges alone; judges can perhaps better control their prejudices.

The other proposals, however, seem to me far too wholesale and ruthless. If, as claimed, they are aimed at organised criminal groups, why should other suspected persons have to be exposed to the incidental risks of police pressure and duress, and to the risk of wrongful conviction? Our cardinal principle is still that an accused is innocent until he is proved guilty. Some of the protections threatened with abolition are aimed, not only against forced self-incriminations, but even more, against false confessions being extracted by such means, leading to miscarriage of justice. Before we lightly destroy these safeguards, each of us should remember that we may ourselves someday be unjustly accused.

If relaxations of the old rules are needed for organised crime, prior sanction from a judge or other high level independent official should be required, after police or prosecution have persuaded him that organised criminality is probably involved.

About the same time as these English proposals are being made, the United States Supreme Court, by a majority of five to four, has held the death penalty unconstitutional. The effect will be to reprieve, but certainly not to release, more than 600 prisoners waiting in so-called 'death rows' all over the country. But of the majority of five, only three judges wholly ruled out the death penalty as being 'a cruel and unusual punishment'. The others only condemned it as such when it is randomly inflicted at the discretion of judges or juries. States wishing to preserve the death penalty may still, for the future, get around the decision by statutes clearly specifying the cases when it may or must be inflicted. For such statutes would probably be upheld by the four present minority judges, plus two of the present majority, making a majority of six to three the opposite way.

Nader's Call to House-Train the Corporate Sector

Monday 10 July 1972, News Commentary

One of Ralph Nader's most charming metaphors in his whirlwind mission here last week was his call to all of us to undertake the 'house-training' of corporate industrial enterprise. The 'house' he referred to is the physical environment, and the training is in keeping it clean and salutary for living creatures.

> Ralph Nader, though himself a radical reformer ... stands at an opposite pole to the rebels against the existing order often referred to as 'the radical left'. They attack the existing social order and dream about new ones. Public Citizen Nader ... is trying to show us how, still starting from where we are, we can revitalise the existing order and even perhaps make it beautiful.

The quality of human life, of course, depends on more than how we produce and consume material things. It also involves the shifting of consumer choices away from material things, to services that – like education and the creative arts – enrich personality and conserve and beautify the environment.

Public Citizen Nader is concerned with all these things, like many other activists. What perhaps distinguishes him are two qualities: first his combined role of diagnostician, practical therapist, and teacher; second his insistence that our major ills can be attacked and remedied from within the free enterprise system, even at its present corporate phase.

He has identified, with classic clarity, 'sub-economies' within the system. These are areas of malfunction of the market, wasteful of consumer bargaining power; or areas of 'malproduction', which involve spoliation of the consumer or the environment. These represent economic slack, he thinks, within our existing framework. And he believes that if we are sufficiently vigorous and persistent in 'house-training', the slack could be taken up and there could be a transformation of both the quality of choice and quality of life within the system.

Nader sees it as the task of 'public citizens' to identify and quantify the elements of malfunction and malproduction, and for the law then to implement the social action policies required in each 'sub-economy'. The best known sub-economy is that of the 'short-changed' consumer, 'short-changed' in the wide sense embracing adulterated or useless food, drugs and cosmetics, or deceptive weights, or planned obsolescence, or fraudulent or inflated home or automobile repairs, or wasteful brand advertising. In all of these, the consumer either does not get what he thinks he is buying, or gets it only with a concealed further liability for later costs. Another is the 'controlled market sub-economy' created by the magnitude of corporate power and manifest not only through monopoly and oligopoly, but also by unwarranted appropriation of funds or exemptions, from the public to the corporate sector for instance, through the taxing power. Still another, ironically, Nader terms 'the compulsory consumption sub-economy', meaning the community's 'compulsory consumption' of environmental pollution and hazards to health and safety. Those who create such pollution and hazard diminish the quality of others' life, often for their own profit, and transfer this loss to the general community and its future generations.

As to these pollutions and hazards that diminish the quality of life, the main tasks are to identify and measure the resulting community loss, and to make those people pay for it who commit the wrong or deprive benefit from it. In the other sub-economies of short-changed consumers, market-rigging and unwarranted appropriation of public resources, the task is the converse one, namely to reduce the price to the consumer by ensuring that proper and competitively set standards are maintained.

It is a nice paradox that Ralph Nader, though himself a radical reformer, constantly attacking the great corporations, stands at an opposite pole to the rebels against the existing order often referred to as 'the radical left'. They attack the existing social order and dream about new ones. Public Citizen Nader, if I understand him aright, is trying to show us how, still starting from where we are, we can revitalise the existing order and even perhaps make it beautiful. For his theory of the sub-economies and economic slack suggests how costing and pricing could become basic links between the quality of life in a democratic society, and the maintenance of a free enterprise economy.

China Vetoes Bangladesh Entry to UN

Wednesday 30 August 1972, Notes on the News

Peking China has cast its first veto in the UN Security Council, on the question of Bangladesh's admission to membership.

The world was agog about this time last year with the prospect of the admission of the People's Republic of China to the UN. One big question which both laymen and diplomats were asking was whether this event would give the UN a new lease of life, in accordance with the wishful principle so dear to the heart of the late Dr HV Evatt, that universal membership was the key to universal peace.

When I spoke to you of this last year, I was very sceptical about the idea that China's admission would simplify anything at all for the UN. I said, indeed, that, at the present stage of history, China's entry was likely in some respects to place fresh obstacles in the UN's way.

My main reason is that, at this stage, the Soviet Union and the US were moving towards a degree of accommodation, especially on those matters that they allowed to come to the Security Council. For, of course, they have long excluded the UN from handling the gravest conflicts between them, like Vietnam, the conflicts over Europe symbolised by the NATO and Warsaw Pacts and the Brezhnev doctrine, and of course their nuclear confrontation.

As a result, the UN was moving in 1971 towards a situation where, in non-major conflicts between Washington and Moscow like their taking different sides on the Indo-Pakistan war, it was conceivable that the Security Council might make some constructive decisions, without either of them exercising the veto.

I said last year that I expected that the entry of Peking China as a Security Council member, also armed with a great power veto, would blight these hopes. And this week's events on the issue of admission of Bangladesh to the UN have unfortunately confirmed this expectation.

During the Indo-Pakistan war in 1971, you may remember, Washington at first took a vigorously anti-Indian position and Moscow an anti-Pakistan position. When it was over, Washington came quickly into line among the majority of UN members who have recognised the new state of Bangladesh.

Admission to the UN requires decisions of both the Security Council and the General Assembly. And, when the matter of Bangladesh's entry came to the Security Council, it was quickly clear that the only serious opposition to admission would come, not from the United States, but from the People's Republic of China. After a week or two of delaying tactics, no doubt in an effort to bring Peking round by informal talks, the matter came to a head at the weekend. In the event, it became a bitter diplomatic confrontation between Moscow and Peking. Peking stepped out from its low-keyed role as a 'new boy' learning the UN ropes, and with a fiery 40-minute speech, cast its first veto to block Bangladesh admission.

It is no use at this stage complaining about the arbitrariness of the Great Power veto. It has been in the UN Charter from its very beginning. The Soviet Union has cast well over a hundred vetoes, the United Kingdom and France have each cast several, and even the United States (which has been most proud of its veto-free virtue) cast its first veto last year, alongside the United Kingdom, in a debate on Rhodesia.[1]

It is, moreover, rather pointless to ask why the UN Charter is not amended so as to abolish the Great Power veto. For amendment of the Charter also requires a decision of the Security Council. And against that decision each Great Power would still be entitled to cast a veto. The chances that no Great Power would cast a veto on a decision to amend the Charter by abolishing the veto, are about as good (or as bad) as the chance of snowdrops surviving in hell.

The present Chinese veto is undoubtedly one factor contributing to an apparent snag in the implementation of the Indo-Pakistan Simla Agreement. India's concern is not limited to the matter of Bangladesh. Mrs Gandhi undoubtedly remains very sensitive, as was her father, Jawaharlal Nehru, in his later years, to Chinese pressure along her northern frontiers. In this context, Peking's veto and the Peking delegation now visiting Islamabad are, for India, a sign of much wider and more chronic problems still on the horizon.

Good afternoon to you all, good afternoon.

---

1   Now the Republic of Zimbabwe.

Iceland Claims Wide Fishing Rights

Monday 4 September 1972, Notes on the News

At the weekend, Iceland put into effect unilaterally, an order extending the exclusive zone for her own fishermen, beyond the 12 miles established in earlier conflicts and permitted by earlier agreements. Iceland's Prime Minister warned yesterday that its three gunboats and spotter-aircraft have sighted 60 odd British ships violating the new zone, and that its gunboats would use force if necessary.

These water around Iceland have been embroiled ever since the 1950s in what has been known as the 'cod war' between Iceland and Britain (though good old herring are also involved).

On August 6, 1971, the Icelandic government conveyed to the Geneva meeting, which is preparing the next Law of the Sea Conference in 1972, her intention to claim exclusive fishing rights over her whole continental shelf. She gave 12 months' notice of this to Britain. The shelf of each country is the extension seaward of its landmass, to the point where the seabed drops away into the deep ocean. In Iceland's case this means generally 50 miles, and at some points 70 miles, from her coast.

Both the British and West German fishing industries are deeply involved. According to British spokesmen, the new measure would virtually exclude foreign fisherman from all their customary fishing grounds for cod and herring. More than 20 percent of fish landed in the United Kingdom come from these waters, and up to 100,000 workers in British fishing and related industries would be thrown into distress.

The British government claims that it is not British fishermen, far from the coast, but Icelanders themselves fishing closer in, where the fish breed, who are the real threat to conservation of fish stocks. But you may have noticed that in an ABC documentary on cod this weekend the Reykjavik story puts it the other way around.

How seriously the parties regard this matter is indicated by earlier instances of the cod war. In the last one, after 1958 when Iceland moved to extend her zone from four miles to 12 miles, matters grew so tense that British trawlers defying the 12-mile ban were, as now, afforded naval escorts, to face Iceland's gunboats.

The 1958 crisis was settled by an exchange of Notes of 11 March 1961, by which the UK in general accepted the 12-mile zone. Iceland undertook to give six months' notice before extending her limits any further, and it was agreed that the UK could refer to the International Court, any dispute that arose concerning such extension.

The United Kingdom, on receiving last year's notice of the new extension, challenged the grounds for it. After the abortive negotiations that followed, the UK claimed under the 1961 agreement to be entitled to submit the dispute to the court. Iceland, however, argued that her agreement to submit to the International Court of Justice, and indeed the whole 1961 agreement, had terminated by the lapse of more than ten years because, she said, they had already exhausted their purpose.

Finally, on 14 April this year, Britain submitted the dispute to the court and also asked for an interim order to preserve the status quo in the meanwhile. On 17 August 1972, over Iceland's objections, the court made an interim order allowing British boats to continue to fish, but setting certain quota limits on catches. Questioning the court's legal powers, Iceland is now defying the order by attempting to enforce her new regime. Britain's naval escorts for its fishermen are thus again confronting Iceland's gunboats. What is more, in these cruel waters, Iceland will be banning ships that trespass from use of her ports and facilities.

This kind of issue is likely to become more and more common as technology makes the oceans and ocean beds more exploitable, and indeed exhaustible. Among the most bitter and chronic of these conflicts is that of local fishermen with those of distant fishing states, which is at the centre of the present cod war. We in Australia will certainly face similar conflicts as other fishing fleets join the Japanese and the Soviet around our vast coastlines. Traditionally we have tended to side with Britain in resisting action like Iceland's which expands the zone of national control over surrounding waters. But we do have vast coast lines, and we are not among the states which want to fish or exploit the sea bed in distant waters.

In consequence we may have a lot of hard rethinking to do before the next Law of the Sea Conference in 1973.

Good afternoon to you all, good afternoon.

Hanoi Leaks News of Ceasefire in Vietnam

Tuesday 31 October 1972, Notes on the News

According to Hanoi, but not according to Washington, this is the day for signing the overall ceasefire agreement, to take effect within 24 hours in Vietnam, with guarantees for the sovereignty and integrity of Cambodia and Laos. We know our reaction when told that war had broken out and since the United Nations was founded in 1945, we have even learned to be blasé about the outbreak of wars, provided they aren't too near us.

Screaming headlines about the outbreak of peace – especially in the 23-year-old war in Vietnam, which has cost about a million and a quarter lives in the last ten years – are however still a bit strange to us.

Anyone not feeling joy or relief would be heartless indeed. And anyone who fails to be curious about the timetabling, and the forces at play in the coming end to the war, must really be utterly bored.

Only six months ago North Vietnam, despite the continuing Paris peace talks, committed all its armoured and most other divisions to a three-pronged thrust on the demilitarised zone in the north, on the central highlands and in the south. And this triggered a great escalation of US bombing, including bombing around Hanoi, and a formidably effective US sea blockade. Amazingly, all this followed quickly after Nixon's visit to Peking, which, apart from Moscow, has been Hanoi's chief support.

We now have the further surprise of Moscow itself backing Washington's position about signature, which is that two or three days' further talks are necessary to clear up outstanding matters. Hanoi claims, on the contrary, that today is the day, and that any loose ends are trivial and can be tied up at the ceremony of signature itself.

Before speculating about this last-minute hitch, we may well ask what explains the remarkable success of negotiations even thus far.

On the American side, it is obvious that Nixon has wanted an early prospect of settlement to help his election prospects. But what about the Hanoi side? Wouldn't Hanoi's prospects be better with a dovish President McGovern rather than President Nixon? The answer to this is the opposite of what it might seem. Hanoi's shrewd and realistic leaders realised months ago that the best time to extract maximum concessions from Nixon and his trouble-shooting Kissinger, would be before the presidential election (when there is still some doubt), rather than after the election, when Nixon would be victoriously safe and home. And this would have been the same even if McGovern's chances had been better.

This kind of thinking would also explain why, after respecting the secrecy of the negotiations up to then, Hanoi suddenly broke secrecy last Thursday, leaking the glad tidings around the world, along with a virtually verbatim 1100-word text of the agreement. With the US election barely a fortnight away, and Kissinger still flitting between Washington and Saigon, obviously still in talks with President Thieu, Hanoi wanted the bird in hand, rather than the bush.

President Nixon, on the other hand, had already by this time obtained electoral mileage out of the expectations of an early ceasefire, without a final signing. Hanoi would get the worst of both worlds, having made concessions which helped Nixon's electoral prospects, while Washington's return concessions would still have to be finally negotiated after the election, with a tough Nixon administration newly flushed with electoral victory.

Not that Washington is not having a hard time with President Thieu, who is declaring vehemently in Saigon that any agreement between Washington and Hanoi was 'their affair', and that there would be no peace in Vietnam until he, President Thieu, had signed the agreement.

President Thieu demands, among other things, a United Nations-supervised referendum to set up a committee to organise new presidential elections in South Vietnam, as opposed to the vague provisions of the reported Washington-Hanoi agreement for free democratic elections 'under international supervision.' He mistrusts the Washington-Hanoi agreement for a kind of troika interim government of right wing, left wing and neutralist elements, which was a notorious failure in Laos. And, most impossible of all, he wants the 145,000 North Vietnamese troops now in South Vietnam to go home. And he is not comforted by Hanoi's assurances that neither the communist north nor the anti-communist south, should aim at liquidating the other.

Dr Kissinger was, of course, confident at the weekend that he could bring President Thieu to heel, as well as get Hanoi to talk some more. The fact is, however, that the United States is not now in position to bring Thieu into line quickly, even after it has brought Moscow and Hanoi and even Peking somewhat into line. And the bitterly ironic reason is that the US combat troops have been withdrawn from Vietnam. The 'Vietnamisation' policy, which has withdrawn all American combat forces from the side of the Thieu regime has, by the same token, reduced American power to bring Thieu quickly into line.

More long-term pressure is a different matter. My guess is that Dr Kissinger's prophecy of a 'matter of weeks' will prove right. A ceasefire is impending – but not before the US presidential elections.

Good afternoon to you all, good afternoon.

Index

Index

www.ingramcontent.com/pod-product-compliance
Lightning Source LLC
Chambersburg PA
CBHW080646270326
41928CB00017B/3201